The Meaning of
Irish Place Names

P9-DVP-054

The Meaning of Irish Place Names

James O'Connell

Blackstaff Press

Published by Blackstaff Press, 255A Upper Newtownards Road, Belfast BT4 3JF.
ISBN 0 85640 175 7
Printed in Ireland by Cahill Printers Limited.

Contents

Foreword

Irish place-names have proved more durable almost everywhere in the country than the language from which they originally came. Among other things they refer to families and comment on topography; they draw attention to animals, plants and trees; they recall churches and saints; and they reflect trades and occupations as well as plagues and massacres. It seems a pity that few persons now know their meanings, and so most miss the history that they embody. This little book tries to give the meanings of over 2,300 place-names. It does not pretend to be a work of scholarship. But it may serve as a rough-and-ready guide until one or other of the several scholars of Irish place-names undertakes a similar project. The pioneering work of P. W. Joyce which combined scholarship with high-level popularisation has been for too long without a succession. Irish place-names are more difficult than most to unravel: some are very old; and others have been anglicised inconsistently and arbitrarily. Hopefully these lists will interest both Irish persons and visitors. Its place-names, which embody the Irish language with such vitality, help to make Ireland distinctive among English-speaking countries.

Abbeydorney: Abbey of the descendants of Torna.
Abbeyfeale: Abbey by the river Feale.
Abbeyknockmoy: Abbey of the Hill of Muaidh (woman's name).
Abbeylara: Abbey of the half-rath.
Abbeyleix: Abbey of Laois.
Abbeyshrule: Abbey of the stream.
Achonry: Conaire's field.
Aclare: Ford of the plank.
Acoose (Lake): Lake of the two caves.
Adare: Ford of the oak grove.
Addergoole: Place between two river forks.
Adrigole: Place between two river forks.
Affane: Middle ford.
Aghaboe: Cow field.
Aghada: Long field.
Aghadoe: Field of the two yew trees.
Aghagower: Field of the well.
Aghalane: Wide field.
Aghalee: Li's field.
Aghamarta: Martin's field.
Aghamore: Big field.
Aghavannagh: Field of the middle mountain.
Aghaville: Field of the sacred tree.
Agherton: Field on the low-lying land.
Aghinver: Field of the estuary.
Aghlish: Church.
Aghmacart: Field of the son of Art.
Aghowle: Field of the orchard.
Ahakista: Ford of the treasure.
Ahane: Little ford.

Ahascragh: Ford of the esker.
Aherlow: Valley.
Ahoghill: Ford of the yew trees.
Aille: Cliff.
Alleen: Little cliff.
Allua (Lough): Lua's lake.
Alt: Hillside height; ravine.
Altan (Lough): Lake of the hillock.
Altataggart: Ravine of the priest.
Altnagelvin: High hillside of the sparrows.
Anascaul: River of the hero.
Annabella: Marsh of the sacred tree.
Annaclone: Marsh of the meadow.
Annacloy: Ford of the stone.
Annacotty: Ford of the small boat.
Annagassan: Ford of the paths.
Annagh: Marsh.
Annaghaskin: March of the eels.
Annaghdown: Marsh of the fort.
Annaghmore: Great marsh.
Annahilt: Marsh of the doe.
Annahone: Eoghan's marsh.
Annakisha: Ford of the wickerwork causeway.
Annalong: Ford of the ships.
Annamoe: Ford of the cows.
Annayalla: Bright marshes.
Anny: Marsh.
Antrim: One clan or house? Elder tree? (meaning is uncertain).
Anure (Lake): Lake of the yew trees.
Ardagh: High field.

Ardamine: Height of the river-forks.

Ardara: Height of the ring-fort.

Ardaragh: Height of oaks.

Ardboe: Height of cows.

Ardcath: Height of the battle.

Ardcroney: Cron's height.

Ardee: Ferdia's ford.

Ardeen: Little height.

Ardfert: Height of the grave.

Ardfinnan: St. Fionan's height.

Ardglass: Glas' height or green height.

Ardglassan: Height of linnets.

Ardgoul: High fork.

Ardgroom: Two ridges (another possible meaning: Height of gloom).

Ardkeen: Pleasant height.

Ardkill: High wood or church.

Ardleckna: Height of the hillside.

Ardlougher: Height of the rushes.

Ardmillan: Height of the mill.

Ardmore: Great height.

Ardnacrusha: Height of the cross.

Ardnagashel: Height of the stone forts.

Ardnageeha: Height of the wind.

Ardnaglas: Height of the feats.

Ardnamona: Height of the bog.

Ardnarea: Height of the executions.

Ardnaree: Height of the kings.

Ardnasodan: Height of the wild ducks.

Ardnurcher: Ford of the cast or throw.

Ardoyne: Eoghan's heights.

Ardpatrick: Height of St. Patrick.

Ardrahan: Height of the ferns.

Ardress: Height of the brambles.

Ards Peninsula: Peninsula of the heights.

Ardscull: Height of the schools (possible: Height of the scolbs or thatching sticks).

Ardskeagh: Height of bushes.

Ardtole: Tuathal's height.

Arigna: Destroyer (name of a river).

Arless: High ring-fort.

Armagh: Macha's height (Macha was a legendary/historical queen).

Armoy: Eastern plain.

Artane: Aidhean's height.

Artigarvan: Height of the house of Garvan.

Artimacormack: Height of the house of the son of Cormac.

Artrea: Height of St. Trea.

Askeaton: Geibhtine's waterfall.

Assey: Sithe's ford.

Athassel: Ford of the fall or stumble.

Athboy: Yellow ford.

Athenry: Ford of the king.

Athgoe: Gon's ford (another possible meaning: Ford of the smith).

Athleague: Ford of the standing stones.

Athlone: Luan's ford.

Athy: Ae's ford.

Attavally: Place of the town.

Atticonaun: Place of the house of Conan.

Aughall: Yew wood.

Augher: Border or verge.
Aughnacloy: Field of the stone.
Aughnaleck: Field of the flagstones.
Aughnanure: Field of the yew trees.
Aughrim: Ridge of the horses.
Avalbane: White orchard.
Ayle: Cliff.

Balbriggan: Brigan's townland.
Baldonnell: Donal's townland.
Baldoyle: Townland of the black foreigners.
Baldungan: Donegan's town (another possible meaning: Townland of the fort).
Balla: Well.
Ballacolla: Town of the hard land.
Ballagh: Road or way, pass.
Ballaghaderreen: Way of the little oak wood.
Ballaghbeama: Pass of the cut or blow.
Ballaghisheen: Oisin's pass.
Ballaghlea: Grey road.
Ballaghmore: Great pass.
Ballickmoyler: Townland of the son of the servant of Mary.
Ballina: Mouth of the ford.
Ballinboy: Mouth of the yellow ford.
Ballinaclash: Townland of the trench.
Ballinaclogh: Townland of the stones.
Ballinaclogher: Townland of the stone buildings.
Ballinacor: Townland of the weir.
Ballinadee: Townland of the cauldron or hollow.
Ballinafad: Mouth of the long ford.

Ballinagar: Ford-mouth of the cars.
Ballinahinch: Townland of the river-meadow.
Ballinakill: Townland of the church.
Ballinalack: Ford-mouth of the flagstones.
Ballinalee: Ford-mouth of the calves.
Ballinamallard: Ford-mouth of the curses.
Ballinamore: Mouth of the big ford.
Ballinamuck: Ford-mouth of the pigs.
Ballinascarthy: Ford-mouth of the thicket.
Ballinasloe: Ford-mouth of the hosting.
Ballinchalla: Townland of the stone buildings.
Ballincloghan: Townland of the stepping-stones.
Ballincollig: Townland of the boar.
Ballincurry: Townland of the marsh.
Ballinderreen: Townland of the small oak groves.
Ballinderry: Townland of the oak groves.
Ballindine: Townland of the small stream.
Ballindooly: Townland of the dark warrior.
Ballindoon: Townland of the fort.
Ballineanig: Townland of the fair.
Ballineddan: Townland of the small stream.
Ballineen: Finin's ford-mouth.
Ballingarry: Townland of the enclosed garden.
Ballingurteen: Townland of the small field.
Ballinlass: Townland of the ring-fort.
Ballinlough: Townland of the lake.
Ballin Prior: The prior's townland.
Ballinrobe: Town of the river Robe.
Ballinskelligs: Townland of Skellig's island.
Ballinspittle: Townland of the hospital.
Ballintaggart: Townland of the priest.

Ballintober: Townland of the well.

Ballintogher: Townland of the causeway.

Ballintra: Townland of the river-meadow.

Ballinure: Townland of the yew tree.

Ballinvally: Townland of the way or road.

Ballitore: Ford-mouth of the bleach-green.

Ballivor: Iomhar's townland.

Balloo: Lugh's townland.

Ballough: Road or way.

Ballyaghagan: Eochagan's townland.

Ballyagalish: Townland of the church.

Ballyard: High townland.

Ballybarrack: Balrac's town.

Ballybay: Ford-mouth of the birch tree.

Ballybeg: Small town.

Ballybetagh: Town of the hospitaller.

Ballybofey: Townland of Fiach's cows.

Ballyboggan: Boggan's townland.

Ballyboghill: Townland of the crozier.

Ballybogy (Ballybogey): Townland of the bog.

Ballybrannagh: Walsh's townland.

Ballybritt: Briotach's townland.

Ballybrittas: Townland of the brattice (another possible meaning: speckled townland).

Ballybrophy: Brophy's townland.

Ballybunion: Bunion's townland.

Ballycahill: The road to Achaille (another possible meaning: O'Cahill's townland).

Ballycanew: Conway's townland.

Ballycarney: Carney's townland.

Ballycarry: Townland of the weir.

Ballycastle: Townland of the castle or stone fort.
Ballyclare: Road of the plain.
Ballycloghan: Townland of the stepping stones.
Ballyclough: Townland of the stone fort.
Ballycolla: Colla's townland.
Ballyconneely: O'Conneely's townland.
Ballyconnell: Conal's ford-mouth.
Ballyconnellan: Connellan's townland.
Ballycormick: Cormac's townland.
Ballycotton: Townland of the common (another possible meaning: Cottin's townland).
Ballycowan: Townland of the son of Aibhne.
Ballycrossaun: Crossan's townland.
Ballycrovane: Mouth of the white marsh.
Ballycroy: Townland of the summit.
Ballycullun: O'Collan's townland.
Ballydaheen: Little David's townland.
Ballydangan: Townland of the fort.
Ballydavis: Daithi's or David's townland.
Ballydehob: Entrance of the two mouths.
Ballydesmond: Desmond's townland.
Ballydooley: O'Dooley's townland.
Ballydownfine: Townland of the fair fort.
Ballyduff: Black townland.
Ballyduggan: O'Duggan's townland.
Ballyeaston: Austin's townland.
Ballyfarnan: Townland of the alder wood.
Ballyfeard: Road of the high wood.
Ballyferriter: Ferriter's townland.
Ballyforan: Ford-mouth of the river-meadow.
Ballyfore: Cold townland.

Ballygally: Geithlech's townland.

Ballygar: Ford-mouth of the enclosed garden (other possible meanings: ford-mouth of the cars; short townland).

Ballygarret: Gearoid's townland.

Ballygawley: O'Daly's townland.

Ballyglass: Green townland.

Ballyglunin: Gluinin's ford-mouth.

Ballygomartin: Townland of Martin's enclosure.

Ballygowan: MacGowan's townland (townland of the son of the smith).

Ballygrogan: Grogan's townland.

Ballyhaise: Eis' ford-mouth (also O'Hea's townland).

Ballyhalbert: Talbot's townland.

Ballyhale: Haol's townland.

Ballyhaunis: Ford-mouth of the battle or plundering.

Ballyhay: Pass of the ford (this name can also mean: O'Hea's townland).

Ballyhean: Ford-mouth of the bird.

Ballyheige: O'Tadhg's townland.

Ballyhooly: Townland of the ford of the apples.

Ballyhornan: O'Fearnan's townland.

Ballyhoura: Feabhrat's townland.

Ballyhusty: Hoiste's townland.

Ballyiriston: Irestan's townland.

Ballyjamesduff: Black James' townland.

Ballykeel: Narrow townland.

Ballykeenan: O'Keanan's townland.

Ballykeeran: Road of the rowan trees.

Ballykelly: O'Kelly's town.

Ballykilleen: Townland of the monk's cell.

Ballykinlar: Townland of the candlestick.
Ballyknock: Townland of the hill.
Ballyknockan: Townland of the little hill.
Ballylanders: Lander's townland.
Ballylarkin: Larkin's townland.
Ballylesson: Townland of the small forts.
Ballylickey: Ford-mouth of the flagstones.
Ballyliffin: Liffin's townland.
Ballylig: Townland of the standing stone.
Ballyline: O'Flynn's townland.
Ballylongford: Ford-mouth of the fortress.
Ballylooby: Ford-mouth of the river loops.
Ballylough: Townland of the lake.
Ballylumford: Townland of the long fiord.
Ballylynen: O'Lynan's townland.
Ballymacallion: Townland of the son of Allion.
Ballymacarbery: Townland of the son of Cairbre.
Ballymacarrett: Townland of the son of Carrett.
Ballymachugh: Townland of the son of Hugh.
Ballymacoda: Townland of the son of Oda.
Ballymagarry: Townland of the enclosed garden.
Ballymagorry: Townland of the son of Gorry.
Ballymahon: O'Mahon's townland.
Ballymakeery: Townland of the son of Ire.
Ballymalis: Malas' ford-mouth.
Ballymartin: Martin's townland.
Ballymascanlan: Townland of the son of Scanlan.
Ballymena: Middle town.
Ballymoe: Mo's ford-mouth.
Ballymoney (Antrim): Townland of the moorland.
Ballymoney (Wexford): Townland of the shrubbery.

Ballymoon: Muna's way or road.

Ballymore: Big townland.

Ballymoreeustace: Big townland of the Eustaces.

Ballymote: Townland of the mound.

Ballymullavill: O'Maolabhal's ford-mouth.

Ballymullen: O'Mullan's townland (there are several Ballymullens — occasionally as in Kerry it means 'Townland of the mill' and as in Laois 'Ford-mouth of the mill').

Ballymurphy: Murphy's townland.

Ballymurray: Murray's townland.

Ballynabarna: Townland of the gap.

Ballynabola: Townland of the summer pasture.

Ballynaboley: Townland of the summer pasture.

Ballynacarrick: Townland of the rock.

Ballynacarriga: Townland of the rock.

Ballynacarrow: Townland of the quarter.

Ballynacarry: Townland of the standing stone.

Ballynacorra: Townland of the weir.

Ballynafeigh: Townland of the exercise green or playing field.

Ballynafid: Townland of the little stream.

Ballynagall: Townland of the foreigners.

Ballynagore: Ford-mouth of the goats.

Ballynahinch: Townland of the river-meadow.

Ballynahown: Townland of the river.

Ballynalackan: Townland of the hillside.

Ballynamona: Townland of the bog.

Ballynapark: Townland of the field.

Ballynaraha: Townland of the fort.

Ballynaskeagh: Townland of the whitethorn bushes.

Ballynastuckaun

Ballynastuckaun: Town of the tree stumps.
Ballyneety: White's townland.
Ballynoe: New town.
Ballynure: Townland of the yew tree.
Ballyporeen: Poreen's ford-mouth.
Ballyragget: Raghat's ford-mouth.
Ballyraheen: Townland of the small ring-fort.
Ballyrashane: Townland of John's fort.
Ballyroe: Russet townland.
Ballyronan: O'Ronan's townland.
Ballyroney: O'Runai's townland.
Ballysadare: Townland of the waterfall of the oak.
Ballyshannon: Seanach's ford-mouth.
Ballyshrule: Townland of the stream.
Ballysillan: Townland of the willow groves.
Ballysimon: Simon's ford-mouth.
Ballysteen: O'Istiadhan's townland.
Ballytrasna: Transverse townland.
Ballyvaughan: O'Behan's townland.
Ballyvourney: Townland of the stony place.
Ballyvoyle: O'Boyle's townland.
Ballywalter: Walter's townland.
Ballywillin: Townland of the mill.
Balrath: Townland of the ring-fort.
Balrothery: Townland of the knight.
Baltimore: Townland of the big house.
Baltinglass: Cuglas' way or road.
Baltray: Townland of the strand.
Banagher: Place of pointed hills.
Bangor: Place of pointed hills.
Bangorerris: Pointed hill place of Erris.

Bannow: Harbour of the suckling pig (banbh).
Bansha: Level grassy place.
Banteer: White country.
Bantry: Descendants of Beann.
Barna: Gap.
Barnaderg: Red gap.
Barnageera: Summit of the sheep.
Barnagh: Gapped.
Barnatra: Top of the strand.
Barnes: Gap.
Barnesmore: Great Gap.
Barraduff: Black top.
Batterstown: Townland of the road.
Bawnboy: Yellow bawn or field.
Bawnmore: Big bawn or field.
Beagh (Lough): Birch lake.
Bealaha: Ford-mouth.
Bealdarrig: Red mouth.
Bedlam: May (place where May festivities were held).
Belclare: Mouth of the plain.
Belcoo: Mouth of the hound (another possible meaning: ford-mouth of the channel or narrow neck).
Belderry: Dearg's estuary.
Belfast: Mouth of the ford of the sandbanks.
Belgooly: Mouth or entrance of the hill-shoulder.
Bellacorick: Ford-mouth of the confluence.
Bellaghy: Mouth of the slough (another possible meaning: Eachadh's townland).
Bellanagare: Ford-mouth of the cars.
Bellanagh: Ford-mouth of the horses.

15

Bellanaleck: Way of the flagstone.
Bellanamullia: Ford-mouth of the blows.
Bellarena: River-mouth of the queen.
Bellaugh: Entrance to the muddy ground.
Bellavally: Mouth of the pass.
Bellavary: Barcud's ford-mouth.
Belleek: Ford-mouth of the flagstone.
Belleeks: Ford-mouth of the flagstone.
Bellurgan: Town of the strip of land.
Belmullet: Entrance to the Mullet peninsula.
Beltany: May (place where May festivities were held).
Beltra: Entrance to the strand.
Belvelly: Entrance to the pass or road (another possible meaning: 'Ford-mouth of the sacred tree').
Benbo: Peaks of the cow.
Benburb: Rough peak.
Bencollaghduff: Peak of the black boar.
Bencrom: Stooped peak.
Benmore: Great peak.
Bentee: Peak of the fairy hill.
Billis: Sacred trees.
Binnion: Low peak.
Birr: Creeks or watery place; also a narrow low-lying tongue of land.
Blaney: Narrow strip of land.
Blaris: Exposed place.
Blarney: Small field.
Boa Island: Badhbha's Island.
Bogagh: Boggy place.
Boggaun: Boggy place.
Boghadoon: Hut of the fort.

Boheeshil: Low hut.
Boher: Road.
Boheravaghera: Road of the plain.
Boherboy: Yellow road.
Boherbue: Yellow road.
Bohera Phuca: Road of the Puca (Puck, hobgoblin).
Bohereen: Little road.
Boherlahan: Wide road.
Boho: Huts.
Bohola: Comhla's hut.
Boley: Place of summer pasture.
Bonamargy: Mouth of the river Margy.
Boolavonteen: Summer pasture of the little bog.
Booterstown: Townland of the road.
Borris: Borough.
Borris-in-Ossory: Borough in Ossory.
Borrisokane: O'Kane's borough.
Borrisoleigh: O'Luigleigh's borough.
Bouladuff: Black summer pasture.
Bovevagh: Maeve's hut.
Boylagh: Territory of the O'Boyles.
Boyle: Car river?
Brackagh: Speckled place.
Bracklin: Speckled.
Brackloon: Speckled meadow.
Bracknagh: Speckled place.
Brandon: St. Brendan's mountain.
Bray: Hill.
Breaghva: Plain of the wolves.
Breandrum: Evil-smelling ridge.
Bready: Broken land.

17

Breda

Breda: Broken land.
Breedage: Broken land.
Breenagh: Fetid stream.
Brickens: Badger warrens.
Bridia: Prisoners.
Brittas: Speckled land.
Broughshane: Shane's house or farm.
Bruckless: Badger cave.
Bruff: Fortified mansion.
Bruree: Fortified mansion of the king.
Bruslee: Grey dust.
Bullaun: Well in a rock.
Bun: End or bottom: river-mouth.
Bunalty: Bottom of the cliff.
Bunalunn: Bottom of the black birds.
Bunbeg: Small river mouth.
Bunbinnia: Bottom of the peak.
Bunbrosna: Source of the river Brosna.
Bunclody: Mouth of the river Clody.
Buncrana: Mouth of the river Crana.
Bundoran: Mouth of the river Dobhran.
Bundorragha: River-mouth of darkness.
Bundrowes: Mouth of the river Drowes.
Bunduff: Mouth of the river Duff.
Bunmahon: Mouth of the river Mahon.
Bunnahowen: River-mouth.
Bunnyconnellan: Conallan's thicket.
Bunratty: Mouth of the river Ratty.
Bunree: River-mouth of the king.
Burren: Stony district.
Burrishoole: Umhall's borough.

18

Buttevant: Push forward ('Boutes-en-avant': the war-cry of the Barry family).

Cabinteely: Sheila's cabin.
Cabra: Poor land.
Cabragh: Poor land.
Cadamstown: Macadam's townland.
Caha: Showery mountains.
Caherbarnagh: Fort of the gap.
Caherconlish: Fort at the head of the lios.
Caherconree: Curaois fort.
Caherdaniel: Donal's stone fort.
Caherduggan: Duggan's stone fort.
Caherlistrane: Stone fort of the place where corn is fired or burnt off the ear.
Cahermore: Great stone fort.
Cahir (Caher): Circular stone fort.
Cahirciveen: Saidhbhin's stone fort
Cairns: Cairns
Callow: Landing place
Caltra (Caldragh): Burial ground
Camaross: Crooked wood.
Camlin: Crooked line.
Camlough: Crooked lake.
Camolin: Eolang's bend.
Camp: The hollow.
Campile: Head of the creek.
Cappagh: Plot of land
Cappaghbeg: Little plot of land.
Cappaghmore: Large plot of land
Capparoe: Russet plot of land.

Cappoquin

Cappoquin: Conn's plot of land.
Cappyantanvally: Plot of the old homestead.
Cargan: Little rock.
Carhoobeg: Small quarter.
Carland: Rocky land.
Carlow: Four lakes.
Carnalbanagh: Cairn of the Scot.
Carnaross: Cairn of the woods.
Carnbane: White cairn.
Carndonagh: Cairn of the church.
Carnew: Cairn of the victory.
Carnfree: Fraoch's cairn.
Carnlough: Cairn of the lake.
Carnmore: Great cairn.
Carnsore: Cairn of the sandy point.
Carntell: Shaohal's cairn.
Carracastle: Quarter of the stone fort.
Carra Lake: Weir lake.
Carragh (Lough): Weir lake
Carrantuohill: Tuathal's curved mountain (another possible meaning: reversed reaping hook)
Carraroe: Russet rocky land
Carrick: Rock
Carrickbeg: Little rock
Carrickblacker: Rock of the Blacker family
Carrickcarnan: Rock of the little cairn (another possible meaning: Naoi's cairn).
Carrickduff: Black rock.
Carrickfergus: Fergus' rock.
Carrickmacross: Rock of the plain of Ross.
Carrickmore: Big rock.

Carrick-on-Shannon: Weir on the Shannon.

Carrick-on-Suir: Rock of the river Suir.

Carrig: Rock.

Carrigallen: Beautiful rock.

Carrigadrohid: Rock of the bridge.

Carrigafoyle: Rock of the hole.

Carrigaholt: Rock of the fleet.

Carrigahorig: Rock of the meeting.

Carrigahooly: Rock of the fleet.

Carrigaline: O'Laighin's rock.

Carrigallen: Beautiful rock.

Carrigaloe: Rock of the tumult (another possible meaning: Rock of the Lua).

Carrigan: Little rock.

Carriganean: Rock of the bird.

Carriganimma: Rock of the butter.

Carrigans: Little rocks.

Carrigaphooca: Rock of the Puca.

Carrigart: Art's rock.

Carrigatogher: Rock of the causeway.

Carrigkerry: Rock of the sheep.

Carrignavar: Rock of the men.

Carrigogunnell: Rock of the O'Connells.

Carrigrohane: Crochan's rock.

Carrigtohill: Tuathal's rock.

Carrow: A quarter of land (a Norman land division).

Carrowdore: Quarter of the water.

Carrowgowan: Quarter of the smith.

Carrowkeel: Narrow quarter.

Carrowkennedy: Kennedy's quarter.

Carrowmore: Big quarter.

Carrowreagh: Grey quarter.

Carrowreilly: O'Reilly's quarter.

Carrowroe: Russet quarter.

Carrowtober: Quarter of the well.

Carryduff: Black quarter.

Carton: Quarter.

Cashel: Circular stone fort.

Cashelgarran: Stone fort of the grove.

Cashla Bridge: Bridge of the sea-inlet.

Castlebar: Barry's castle.

Castlecomer: Castle of the confluence or river bottom.

Castleconnell: O'Conaing's castle.

Castlecoole: Secluded castle (Castle of the recess).

Castlecor: Castle of the weir.

Castlederg: Castle on the river Derg.

Castledermot: Originally: Dermot's hermitage.

Castledillon: Originally: Iolladhan's hermitage.

Castlefinn: Castle of the river Finn.

Castlegal: Bright stone fort.

Castlelyons: O'Lehane's castle.

Castle Kirke: Castle of the hen.

Castleknock: Castle of the hill or mound.

Castlemartyr: Castle of the relics of the martyrs.

Castlemain: Castle on the river Maine.

Castlemoyle: Bare or dilapidated castle.

Castlepook: Castle of the Puca.

Castlerea: Grey castle.

Castlereagh: Grey castle.

Castleroe: Russet castle.

Castleventry: Castle of the winds.

Castlewellan: Uidhilin's castle.
Cavan: The hollow.
Celbridge: Church of the bridge.
Chapelizod: Iosoilde's chapel.
Clabby: Open place.
Claddagh: Sea shore.
Claddaghduff: Black sea shore.
Clady: Ground hardened from trampling; also muddy place.
Claggan: Headland.
Clanabogan: O'Bogan's meadow.
Clandeboye: Descendants of Yellow Aodh (Yellow Hugh O'Neill).
Clane: Slope.
Clankee: Descendants of the one-eyed man (Niall O'Reilly).
Clara: Level place.
Clare: Level land.
Clareen: Small level plain.
Clare-Galway: Originally: Town of the plain.
Claremorris: Plain of the descendants of Muiris.
Clarina: Aidhne's plain.
Clarinbridge: Bridge of the little plank.
Clash: Trench or furrow.
Clashaganny: Sand trench.
Clenor: Dark-grey meadow.
Cliffony: Grove of the hurdles.
Clogh: Stone or stone castle.
Cloghan: Stepping stones.
Cloghanchorca: Stepping stones across the marsh.
Cloghane: Stone house.

Cloghballymore: Stone castle of the big townland.

Clogheen: Little stone castle.

Clogher: Stony place.

Cloghfine: White stone.

Cloghmore: Big stone castle.

Cloghone: Eoghan's stone.

Cloghore: Stone of gold.

Cloghoula: Stone circle.

Cloghpook: Stone of the Puca.

Cloghy: Stony place.

Clonad: Long meadow.

Clonakilty: O'Caoilte's meadow? Meaning is uncertain.

Clonalig: Meadow of the standing stone.

Clonard: Irard's meadow (Co. Meath); elsewhere, high meadow.

Clonaslee: Meadow of the road or pass.

Clonbrock: Meadow of the badgers.

Clonbulloge: Meadow of sacks.

Cloncrew: Meadow of wild garlic.

Cloncullen: Meadow of holly.

Cloncurry: Conaire's meadow.

Clondalkin: Dolcan's meadow.

Clonduff: Meadow of the ox.

Clone: Meadow.

Clonea: Meadow of the deer.

Cloneen: Little meadow.

Clonegall: Meadow of the foreigners.

Clones: Eos' meadow.

Cloney: Meadow.

Clonfad: Long meadow.

Clonfeacle: Meadow of the tooth.
Clonfert: Meadow of the grave.
Clonfinloch: Meadow of the white lake.
Clongowes: Meadow of the smith.
Clonkeen: Pleasant meadow.
Clonlea: Meadow of the calves.
Clonenagh: Meadow of the ivy.
Clongill: Meadow of the foreigner.
Clonmacnoise: Meadow of the son of Nos.
Clonmahon: Descendants of Mahon.
Clonmany: Maine's corner.
Clonmeen: Smooth meadow.
Clonmel: Meadow of honey.
Clonmellon: Miolan's meadow.
Clonmines: Smooth meadow.
Clonmore: Great meadow.
Clonmult: Meadow of the wethers.
Clonoe: Meadow of the yew tree.
Clonony: Damhna's meadow.
Clonroche: Roche's meadow.
Clontarf: Meadow of the bulls.
Clontibret: Meadow of the well.
Clontuskert: Northern meadow.
Clonygowan: Meadow of the descendants of the smith.
Cloonaddra: Meadow between two fords.
Cloonard: High meadow.
Cloonart: Art's meadow.
Cloonbeg: Small meadow.
Cloonboo: Meadow of the victory.
Cloondara: Meadow of the two ring-forts.

Cloone

Cloone: Meadow.
Cloonee: Meadows.
Clooneen: Little meadow.
Clooney: Meadow.
Cloonfad: Long meadow.
Cloonlara: Meadow of the mare.
Cloonlough: Meadow of the mallows (another possible meaning: Lua's meadow).
Cloonmore: Great meadow.
Cloonty: Meadows.
Cloonyquin: O'Quinn's meadow.
Clough: Stone castle.
Cloughboy: Yellow castle.
Cloughey: Stony place.
Cloughjordan: Jordan's castle.
Cloughoughter: Upper castle.
Clounanna: Meadow of the horses.
Clowney: Place of meadows.
Cloyne: Meadow.
Clydagh: Rocky place.
Coa: Windy place.
Coad: Grave.
Coagh: The Hollow.
Cobh: Cove.
Colehill: Hazel wood.
Coleraine: Nook of the ferns.
Colgagh: Prickly place.
Collon: Holly.
Comber: Confluence or river-bed.
Comeragh: Place of confluences.
Commeen: Little valley.

Cong: Isthmus.

Conlig: Flagstone of the hounds.

Conna: Hound wood.

Conmacht: Conn's place.

Connagh: Place abounding in fire-wood.

Conneen: Little corner.

Connello: Territory of the O'Connell Gabhra.

Connemara: The Conmacne people of the sea.

Connonagh: Place of white heads.

Connor: Oakwood of the hounds.

Convoy: Hound plain.

Conwald: Habitation.

Coolagh: Land at the back of the hill or other such place.

Coolaney: Maine's secluded place.

Coolattin: Corner of the gorse.

Coolbanagher: Nook of the pointed hills.

Coolbaun: White corner.

Coolboy: Yellow secluded spot.

Coolderg: Red corner.

Coolderry: Nook of the oak grove.

Cooldrumman: Secluded place of the little hills.

Coole: Corner, secluded place, back place, nook.

Cooley: Corner or nook, secluded place.

Coolgreany: Sunny nook.

Coolhill (Coolkill): Wood at the back.

Coolkenna: O'Cionaoth's corner.

Coolmore: Big secluded place.

Coolooney: Secluded grove.

Coolroe: Reddish-brown corner.

Coolseskin: Back marsh.

Coom (Combe)

Coom (Combe): Hollow, mountain valley.
Coomcallee: Valley of the hag.
Coomlettra: Valley of the hillside.
Coomakista: Valley of the treasure.
Coornagrena: Curved hollow of the sun.
Coornameana: Curved hollow of the gorge.
Coos (Coose): Cave.
Coosan (Coosane, Cossaun): Little cave.
Coppanagh: Place abounding in dock leaves.
Corbally: Odd townland.
Corbeagh: Round hill of the birch.
Corbollis: Odd townland.
Corcaghan: Marshy place.
Corclough: Round hill of the stones.
Corcomroe: The people of Modhruadh.
Cordangan: Fortified round hill.
Cordarragh: Round hill of the oak tree.
Corgarry: Round hill of the garden.
Corglass: Green round hill.
Cork: Marsh.
Corlacky: Hill of flagstones.
Corlea (Corrlea): Grey round hill.
Cornafulla: Round hill of the blood.
Cornakill: Round hill of the church.
Cornagee (Cornageeha): Round hill of the wind.
Cornahoe: Round hill of the cave.
Cornamona: Round hill of the bog.
Cornaveagh: Round hill of the ravens.
Corr: Round hill.
Corraun: Sickle-shaped.
Corrauntoohill: Inverted sickle.

Corraclare: Russet round hollow of the plain.
Corraveccan: Round hill of the mushroom.
Corrigeenroe: Little russet rock.
Corrofin: Finn's weir.
Corroy: Russet round hill.
Corvalley: Bend of the road.
Coss: Recess.
Costelloe: Sea inlet.
Coumenare: Valley of the slaughter.
Coumeenoole: Dineal's valley.
Coumshingaun: Valley of the ants.
Courtmacsherry: Residence of the son of Geoffrey.
Craan (Cranne): Stony place.
Crag (Craig): Rock.
Craggagh: Rocky.
Craigalusta: Rock of the kneading-trough or fertile land.
Craigavad: Rock of the boat.
Craigdoo: Black rock.
Cranagh: Place abounding in trees.
Cranfield: Corruption of Gaelic form: wood of the wild garlic.
Crataloe (Ratloe): Willow wood.
Craughwell: Place of plunders (where plunder was kept).
Creagh: Hard place on the edge of soft or marshy land.
Crecora: Sweet-scented branchy tree.
Creeagh: Boundary.
Creeve: Branchy tree.
Creevy: Narrow branchy place.

Creeslough: Lake of gluttony, i.e., lake that swallows things.

Creevagh: Branchy place.

Creevela: Grey branch.

Creevaghmore: Big branchy place.

Cregagh: Rocky place.

Cregg: Rock.

Creggan (Creggane, Creggaun): Rocky place.

Cregganbaun: Small white rocky place.

Crenville: Wood of wild garlic.

Crettyard: High hillocks.

Crilly: Shaky place.

Croagh: Round hill.

Croaghan: Round hill.

Croaghpatrick: Round hill of St. Patrick.

Crockmore: Big hill.

Crolly: Shaking bog.

Cromac: River-bend.

Cromkill: Sloping wood.

Crookhaven: Haven of the round hill.

Croom: Sloping place.

Crossakeel: Cool's crosses (another possible meaning: Slender crosses).

Crossboy: Yellow cross.

Crossderry: Transverse oak grove.

Crossdoney: Cross of the church.

Crossea: Aodh's cross.

Crosserlough: Cross on the lake.

Crossfarnoge: Cross of the elder bushes.

Crossgar: Short cross.

Crossmaglen: Cross of the son of Lionnan.

Crossmolina: Cross of Maolfhina.
Crove: Round hill of the birch (another possible meaning: Birch enclosure).
Crowhill: Hard wood.
Crumlin: Curved glen.
Crusheen: Little cross.
Cuilbeg: Little wood.
Culdaff: Back of the flax dam (another possible meaning: Dabhcha's secluded spot).
Culkey: Place abounding in weeds.
Cullahill: Back wood.
Cullaville: Townland of the son of Cullach.
Culleens: Little woods.
Cullinagh: Sloping place.
Cullingtree: Place abounding in holly.
Cully: Woodland.
Cullybackey: Wood of the hollow.
Cultra: Secluded strand.
Cumber (Cummer): Confluence, river-bed.
Cummeenduff: Black river valley.
Curra: Marsh.
Currabaha: Birch marsh.
Currabeha: Bithe's weir (another possible meaning: birch marsh).
Curracloe: Lo's marsh.
Curraflugh: Wet marsh.
Curragh: Marsh, moorland.
Curragh (Kildare): Race-course, level moorland.
Curraghbeg: Little marsh.
Curraghbinny: Marsh of the peak.

Curraghboy: Yellow marsh.
Curraghderg: Dearg's marsh.
Curraghduff: Black marsh.
Curraghlahan (Curraghlane): Broad marsh.
Curraghmore: Great marsh.
Curraheen: Little marsh.
Curran: Sickle-shaped.
Curraun: Sickle-shaped, curved.
Currikippane: Moor of the tree trunks.
Curryglas: Grey marsh, grey weir.
Cush: Foot (at the foot of...).
Cushendall: Bottom of the river Dall.
Cushendun: Bottom of the river Dun (brown river).
Cutteen: Commonage.

Dacklin: Black meadow.
Daingean: Fortress.
Dalkey Island: Thorn island (Anglicised version of Scandinavian name which translated an Irish name).
Dalway's Bawn: Dalway's fortified farmhouse.
Dangan: Fortress.
Dargle: Little red spot.
Darragh: Place abounding in oaks.
Darraragh (Darrey): Place abounding in oaks.
Dawros: Ox wood or peninsula.
Deelis (Deelish): Black ring-fort.
Deereeny: Little oak grove.
Delgany: Little red spot (another possible meaning: thorny place).
Delvin: Descendants of Dealbhaeth.

Derralossary: Losar's oak grove.

Derreen: Little oak grove.

Derrinturn: Oak grove of the kiln.

Derry: Oak wood or grove.

Derryard: High oak grove.

Derrybawn: White oak grove.

Derrybeg: Oak grove.

Derrybrien: Braon's oak grove.

Derryclare: Oak grove of the plain.

Derrycoush: Oak grove of the cave.

Derrycreevy: Oak grove of the branches.

Derrygarriff (Derrygarve): Rough oak grove.

Derrygeel: Oak grove of the Gaels or Irish.

Derrygonnelly: Oak grove of the O'Connollys.

Derryharney: Oak grove of the O'Kearneys.

Derryhivenny: Oak grove of the river.

Derrykeighan: Keegan's oak grove.

Derrylee: Li's oak grove.

Derrylester: Oak grove of the cup.

Derrylin: Flann's oak grove.

Derrymore: Big oak grove.

Derrynacreebe: Oak grove of the cattle.

Derrynacreeve: Oak grove of the clay (other possible meanings: oak grove of the branchy trees; wood of the wild garlic).

Derrynafeana: Oak grove of the Fianna (legendary heroes).

Derrynahinch: Oak grove of the island or river-meadow.

Derrynamuck: Oak grove of the pigs.

Derrynane: Fionnan's oak grove.

Derryneen: Finin's oak grove.
Derryquay: Oak grove of the son of Aodh.
Derrytrasna: Transverse oak grove.
Derryveagh: Birch wood.
Dervock: Little oak grove.
Desert: Hermitage, secluded place.
Desertmartin: St. Martin's hermitage.
Desertmore: Great hermitage.
Devenish: Ox island.
Diamor: A solitude.
Dingle: Fortress (of O'Cush).
Divis: Black hill.
Doagh: Sand hill.
Donabate: Church of the boat.
Donacarney: Church of the cairn.
Donagh: Church.
Donaghadee: Church of St. Diach.
Donaghcloney: Church of the meadow.
Donaghmore: Large church.
Donagh Patrick: Church of St. Patrick.
Donard: High ring-fort.
Donegal: Fort of the foreigners.
Donegore: Church or fort of the warriors.
Doneraile: Fort on a cliff.
Donnybrook: Church of St. Broc.
Donohill: Fort of the yew wood.
Donore: Fort of pride.
Donoughmore: Large church.
Dooagh: Sand bank.
Doochary: Black weir.
Doogary: Black garden.

Dooish: Black hill.

Dooks: Dunes.

Doo Lough: Black lake.

Doon: Fort.

Doonaha: Fort of the ford.

Doonamo: Fort of the cows.

Doonan: Little fort.

Doonard: High fort.

Doonbeg: Small fort.

Doonisky: Fort of water.

Doonooney: Una's fort.

Dore: Water.

Dorsey: Doors.

Douglas: Black stream.

Down: Fort.

Downings: Little forts.

Downpatrick: Fort of St. Patrick.

Downs: Forts.

Dowra: River-meadow of the oxen.

Dreen: Blackthorn.

Dreenagh: Place of blackthorns.

Drimna: Place of ridges.

Drimoleague: Ridge of the two standing stones.

Drinagh: Place of blackthorns.

Drinnahilly: Ridge of the willows.

Dripsey: Muddy river.

Drishane: Bushes; little brambly place.

Drogheda: Bridge of the ford.

Dromada: Long ridge.

Dromahair: Ridge of the two demons.

Dromaneen: Little ridge.
Dromantine: Hill of the foxglove.
Dromara: Heifer ridge.
Dromard: High ridge.
Drombeg: Little ridge.
Dromcolliher: Ridge of the hazel wood.
Dromdorry: Ridge of the black oak grove.
Dromin: Little ridge.
Dromineer: Ridge of the river mouth.
Drominskin: Ineasclann's ridge.
Dromkeen: Pleasant ridge.
Dromluska: Burnt ridge.
Drommartin: Martin's ridge.
Dromond: Long ridge.
Dromore: Great ridge.
Dromstabla: Ridge of the stable.
Dromud: Long ridge.
Drumacoo: Hound ridge.
Drumahoe: Ridge of the mist.
Drumbo: Cow ridge.
Drumcar: Ridge of the weir.
Drumcard: Ridge of the craftsmen.
Drumcliff: Ridge of the baskets.
Drumclose: Ridge of hollows or caves.
Drumcondra: Contra's ridge.
Drumconnick: Conmhac's ridge.
Drumconrath: Conra's ridge.
Drumcree: Ridge of cattle.
Drumcrin: Ridge of the trees.
Drumcroon: Ridge of the Picts.

Drumderg: Red ridge.
Drumfad: Long ridge.
Drumfinn: Fair ridge.
Drumfree: Heather ridge.
Drumgarriff: Rough ridge.
Drumgoff: Stone ridge.
Drumgrenaghan: Greinachan's ridge.
Drumhallagh: Ridge of willows.
Drumharriff: Bull ridge.
Drumhillagh: Ridge of willows.
Drumkeen: Pleasant ridge.
Drumkeeran: Ridge of rowan trees.
Drumlane: Broad ridge.
Drumlave: Ridge of elm trees.
Drumlish: Ridge of the ring-fort.
Drumnacros: Ridge of the cross.
Drumnakilly: Ridge of the church.
Drumnaraw: Ridge of the ring-fort.
Drumneechy: Naoise's ridge.
Drumod: Long ridge.
Drumquin: Pleasant ridge.
Drumraney: Ridge of ferns.
Drumreagh: Gray ridge.
Drumree: Ridge of the king.
Drumsallagh: Miry ridge.
Drumshallon: Ridge of the gallows.
Drumshanbo: Ridge of the old cow.
Drumsna: Ridge on the swimming place.
Drumsurn: Ridge of the kiln.
Drung: Multitude or crowd; a meeting place.

Duagh: Black ford.
Dublin: Black pool (the usual name in Gaelic is Baile Atha Cliath which is 'town of the ford of the hurdles').
Dufferin: The black third-part.
Duhallow: District of the river Allo.
Dulane: Little hill.
Duleek: Stone house or church.
Dunadry: Middle or central fort.
Dunamase: Fort of Masc.
Dunamon: Iomgan's fort.
Dunboy: Yellow fort.
Dunboyne: Baethan's fort.
Dunbrody: Bruide's fort.
Duncannon: Ceanann's fort.
Duncormick: Cormac's fort.
Dundalk: Dealgan's fort.
Dunderrow: Fort of the oak plain.
Dunderry: Fort of the oak grove.
Dundonald: Donal's fort.
Dundrum: Fort of the ridge.
Dunfanaghy: Fort of Finn Chu (another possible meaning: Fort of the white field).
Dungannon: Ceanann's fort.
Dungarvan: Garbhan's fort.
Dungiven: Fort of the hide.
Dungloe: Fort of the tumult.
Dunheeda: Sioda's fort.
Dunhill: Fort of the cliff.
Dunkettle: Cital's fort.

Dunlaoghaire: Laoghire's fort.

Dunleer: Fort of austerity (another possible meaning: Leri's fort).

Dunlevy: Lughach's fort.

Dunloe: Fort of the river Loe/Fort of water.

Dunluce: Fort or ring-fort.

Dunmanus: Manas' fort.

Dunmanway: Fort of (the land of) the Manmha.

Dunmore: Great fort.

Dunmurry: Muireadach's fort.

Dunnamanagh: Fort of the monks.

Dunquin: Pleasant fort.

Dunsandle: Sandal's fort.

Dunseverick: Sobhaire's fort.

Dunshaughlin: Church of St. Seachlann.

Dunsink: Sineach's fort.

Dunsoghly: Sochaille's fort.

Duntryleague: Fort of the three standing stones.

Durrow: Oak plain.

Durrus: Black wood.

Dysert: Isolated place, hermitage.

Dysartenos: Hermitage of St. Aongus.

Dysert O'Dea: Hermitage of O'Dea.

Easky: Place abounding in fish.

Eden: Hill-brow or slope.

Edenderry: Hill-brow of the oak grove.

Edenmore: Great hill-brow.

Edentinny: Hill-brow of fire.

Ederny: Middle area.

Eglish

Eglish: Church.

Eighter: Lower area.

Ellistrin: Place abounding in flaggers (type of small fly).

Elphin: Rock of the clear spring.

Emlagh: Marshy lake.

Emlaghdauroe: Marsh of the two red cows.

Emly: Lake marsh of the yew tree.

Emlygrennan: Lake marsh of the sun-bower.

Emyvale: Vale of the bed.

Ennis: River-meadow.

Enniscrone: River-meadow of the esker.

Enniskean: Pleasant river-meadow (another possible meaning: Cian's river-meadow).

Enniskerry: Fort of the rocky crossing.

Enniskillen: Cethle's island.

Ennisnag: River-meadow of the woodpecker.

Ennistymon: Dioman's river-meadow.

Errigal: A habitation; a small church or oratory.

Errigal Keeroge: Oratory of St. Dachiarog.

Eshnadarragh: Ridge of the oakwood.

Eskeragh: Place of eskers.

Eyries: Rising ground.

Faha: Exercise green.

Fahan: Slope.

Falcarragh: Rough hedge.

Fallmore: Great enclosures.

Falls: Enclosures or hedges enclosing land.

Fanad: Sloping ground.

Farahy: Parish

Farnagh: Place of alders.
Farney: Plain of alders.
Farran: Land.
Farrancassidy: O'Cassidy's land.
Farranfore: Cold land.
Feagh: Woody place.
Feakle: Tooth.
Fee (Lough): Lake of the wood.
Feeard: High wood.
Feenagh: Place of woods.
Feeny: Place of woods.
Fenit: Wild place.
Fenor: White spot.
Feohanagh: Place of thistles.
Ferbane: Whitish grass.
Fermanagh: Men of Monach.
Fermoy: (Monastery of) the men of the plain.
Ferns: Place of alders.
Ferrycarrig: Grey rock.
Fertagh: Place of graves.
Fethard: High wood.
Fews: Woods.
Fiddown: Wood of the fort.
Fieries: Woods.
Finaghy: White field.
Fingall: Land of the foreigners.
Finglas: White stream.
Finnea: Wood of the ford.
Finnihy River: Deer stream.
Fintona: Fair-coloured field.
Fintown: Town of the river Finn.

Fintragh

Fintragh: White strand.
Finvoy: White hut.
Flesk: Well or bog.
Foil: Cliff.
Fore: Spring.
Forenaght: Bare cold hill.
Four Knocks: Cold hill.
Foy: Exercise green.
Foyle: Cliff or estuary.
Foynes: Western boundary.
Freshford: Fresh field ('Ford' was a mistaken translation).
Freughmore: Great heath.
Frosses: Showers.
Funshine: Place of ash trees.
Fussough: Sheltered place.

Galbally: Townland of the foreigners.
Galwally: Townland of the foreigners.
Gallavally: Summer-pasture of the foreigners.
Gallen: Dishonoured spear (sobriquet for a particular chief).
Galtee Mountains: Mountains of the woods.
Galway: Gailleamh's place.
Garbally: Short townland or rough townland.
Gardrum: Short ridge.
Garinish: Near island.
Garnavilla: Grove of the sacred tree.
Garrane: Shrubbery, grove.
Garryduff: Black garden.
Garrymore: Great garden.

Garryowen: Eoghan's garden.

Garryspillane: Spealan's garden.

Gartan: Small field.

Garvagh: Rough place.

Garvaghy: Rough field.

Garvarry: Rough land.

Gearhameen: Smooth river-grove.

Geashill: Place of swans.

Gill (Lough): Bright lake.

Gilnahirk: (Hill brow of the) gillie of the horn (horn-blower).

Glanbehy: Glen of the birch trees.

Glandore: Dor's harbour.

Glanerdalliv: Glen of the high land.

Glanleam: Glen of the leap.

Glanmire: Maghar's glen.

Glanmore (Lough): Lough of the large glen.

Glantane: Little glen.

Glanworth: Watery glen.

Glasdrummond: Green ridge.

Glasheen: Little stream.

Glaslough: Grey lake.

Glasnevin: Naeidhe's stream.

Glassan: Little stream.

Glassillan: Green island.

Glenaan: Little glen.

Glenade: Eada's glen.

Glenagarey: Glen of the sheep.

Glenamoy: Valley of the river Moy.

Glenanaar: Glen of the slaughter.

Glenanair: Glen of the slaughter.

Glenariff: Glen of the arable land.

Glenarm: Glen of the weapon or army.

Glenart: Art's glen.

Glenavuddig: Glen of the churl.

Glenavy: Church of the dwarf.

Glenballyemon: Glen of Eamonn's townland.

Glenbane: White glen.

Glenbeigh: Glen of the birch trees.

Glencam: Crooked glen.

Glencar: Carthac's glen (another possible meaning: Glen of the rock).

Glencar: Glen of the standing stone (Glencar Lake).

Glencloy: Glen of the fences (another possible meaning: glen of the fort).

Glencorp: Glen of the slaughtered.

Glencorrib: Valley of the Corrib.

Glencree: Shaky glen.

Glencullen: Glen of the holly.

Glendalough: Glen of the two lakes.

Glendine: Deep glen.

Glendowan: Deep glen.

Glendun: Glen of the river Dun (also: glen of the fort).

Gleneask: Glen of the fish.

Gleneely: Daol's glen.

Glengarriff: Rugged glen.

Glengavlen: Glen of the fork.

Glengormley: Gormley's glen (another possible meaning: Gormley's family).

Gleninagh: Glen of the ivy.

Glenkeen: Pleasant glen.

Glenlossera: Lasrach's glen.

Glenmacnass: Glen of the sons of Neasa.

Glenmalure: Glen of the servant of Iura.

Glenmore: Great glen.

Glennaghevlagh: Glen of the fetters.

Glennahalla: Glen of the Ula or monument.

Glennanean: Glen of the birds.

Glenoe: Glen of the yew tree.

Glenogra: Ogra's glen.

Glenosheen: Oisin's glen.

Glenshane: Sean's glen.

Glenshesk: Glen of the sedges.

Glenstal: Stathel's glen.

Glentaise: Taise's (a king's daughter) glen.

Glentane: Little glen.

Glentavraun: Samhran's glen.

Glenties: Glens.

Glenveagh: Glen of the birch trees.

Glenwhirry: Glen of the whirlpool.

Glin: Glen.

Glynn: Glen.

Gobbins: Rocky point.

Golden: Little fork.

Goleen: Little inlet.

Gorey: Sandbank (another possible meaning: place of horses).

Gort: Tilled field, field.

Gortaclare: Field of the level land.

Gortacurrane: Field of the sharp rocks.

Gortadirra: Field of the oak grove.

Gortagreenane: Field of the sun-bower.

Gortahork: Field of the oats.

Gortalassa: Field of the ring-fort.

Gortavoy: Field of the plain.

Gorteen: Little field.

Gorteeny: Little fields.

Gortin: Little field.

Gortlaoughra: Field of rushes.

Gortmore: Big field.

Gortnagarn: Field of the cairns.

Gortnagross: Field of the crosses.

Gortnamona: Field of the bog.

Gortnaskeagh: Field of the whitethorn bushes.

Gouganebarra: Rocky cave of St. Finnbarr.

Gouldavoher: Fort of the two roads.

Goulnacappy: Fork of the plot.

Graigue: Village.

Graiguenamanagh: Village of the Welsh.

Grallagh: Muddy place.

Granabeg: Little gravelly place.

Grangegeeth: Windy grange.

Grangemockler: Mockler's grange.

Gransha: Grange.

Greenane: Summer dwelling place, sun-bower.

Grevine: Rough place.

Groomsport: Harbour of the gloomy servant.

Gulladuff: Black hill-shoulder.

Gurranabraher: Grove of the friars (another possible meaning: Rocky eminence of the frairs or brothers).

Gurtymadden: Madden's field.

Gweebarra: Barry's tide-inlet.

Gweedore: Dore's tide-inlet.
Gweesalia: Salt-water inlet.
Gyleen: Little fork.

Hyne (Lough): Cauldron lake, lake of the whirlpool.

Idrone: Island of the descendants of Drona.
Illan: Island.
Illaunmore: Great island.
Illauntanning: St. Seanach's island.
Imaal: Land of the descendants of Mal.
Inagh: Place of ivy.
Inch: Island or river-meadow, also sea-meadow (Kerry).
Inchagoill: Island of the foreigner.
Inchicore: Guaire's river-meadow.
Inchicronan (Lake): Lake of the island of St. Cronan.
Inchidoney: Island of the person or individual.
Inchmore: Great island or river-meadow.
Inishannon: Eoghan's river-meadow.
Inishbeg: Little island.
Inishbofin: Island of the white cow.
Inishcarra: Island of the leg.
Inishcealtra: Cealtra's island.
Inishclothran: Clothra's island.
Inishcrone: Crona's island.
Inisheer: Eastern island.
Inishfree: Island of the heather.
Inishkeen: Beautiful island.
Inishmaan: Middle island.
Inishmore: Great island.

Inishmurray

Inishmurray: Murray's island.
Inishowen: Eoghan's island or peninsula.
Inishtioge: Teoc's river-meadow.
Inishtooskert: Northern island.
Inis Patrick: St. Patrick's island.
Inniscarra: See Inishcarra.
Innisfallen: Faithlenn's island.
Innisfree: Island of the heather.
Inver: River mouth.
Isertkelly: Kelly's hermitage.
Island Magee: Island of the son of Hugh.
Island Mahee: St. Mochaoi's island.

Kanturk: Hill of the boar.
Keadew: Flat-topped green hill.
Keady: Pass of the deer.
Kealkill: Narrow wood.
Keam Bridge: Bridge of the pass.
Keel: A narrow place.
Keeloges: Narrow strip or ridge.
Keem: Pass.
Keenagh: Mossy place.
Keenaght: Land of the descendants of Cian.
Keimaneigh: Pass of the deer.
Kenbane: White head.
Kenmare: Head of the sea (highest point reached by the tide).
Kensalebeg: Small sea head.
Kerry: Land of the descendants of Ciar.
Kerrykeel: The narrow quarter.
Kesh: Wickerwork causeway.

Keshcarrigan: Wicker causeway of the little rock.

Kilbaha: Church of the birchwood.

Kilbarrack: Church of St. Berach.

Kilbarron: Church of St. Barron (Barron means fair-haired).

Kilbarry: Church of St. Finnbarr (Finnbarr means fair-haired).

Kilbeggan: Church of St. Beagan.

Kilbeheny: Birch wood.

Kilbolane: Church of St. Bolan.

Kilbonane: Church of St. Bonan.

Kilbrittain: Church of St. Briotan.

Kilbroney: Church of St. Bronach.

Kilcock: Church of St. Coca.

Kilcogy: Church of St. Coige.

Kilcolgan: Church of St. Colga.

Kilconnell: Church of St. Conall.

Kilcoo: Church of St. Cua.

Kilcoolaght: Church of the company or colony.

Kilcoole: Church of St. Comgall.

Kilcooley: Church of the secluded place.

Kilcormac: Church of St. Cormac.

Kilcornan: Church of St. Cornan.

Kilcrea: Church of St. Crea.

Kilcrohane: Church of St. Crochan.

Kilcullen: Church of St. Cuilleann.

Kilcummin: Church of St. Coimin.

Kilcurry: Church of the marsh.

Kildare: Church of the oak grove.

Kildavin: Church of St. Damhan.

Kildemock: Church of St. Deamog.

Kildimo: Church of St. Dioma.

Kildorrery: Church of the oak woods.

Kilfenora: Church of St. Fionnuir.

Kilfinane: Church of St. Fionan.

Kilgobnet: Church of St. Gobnait.

Kilkee: Church of St. Caoidhe.

Kilkeel: Narrow church (other possible meanings: Wattle church, Church of the narrow straits).

Kilkelly: Ceallach's church.

Kilkenny: Church of St. Cainneach.

Kilkieran: Church of St. Ciaran.

Kilkinlea: Church of the mountain.

Kilkishen: Church of the little wicker causeway.

Killala: Church of St. Ala.

Killaloe: Church of St. Dalua.

Killaloo: Wood of the calf.

Killadeas: Church of the Culdees (Culdee means companion of God. Culdees were monastic reformers).

Killadysert: Church of the hermitage.

Killamery: Church of St. Lamhrach.

Killan: Church of St. Anne.

Killane: Church of St. Anne.

Killard: Church of the height.

Killare: Church of the slaughter.

Killarga: Church of St. Fearga.

Killarney: Church of the sloes.

Killary: Narrow sea-inlet.

Killashandra: Church of the old ring-fort.

Killashee: Church of the fairy hill.

Killavally: Church of the way.

Killavullen: Church of the mill.
Killeagh: Church of St. Fiach.
Killeavy: Church of the mountain.
Killeedy: Church of St. Ide.
Killeen: Little woods.
Killeenagh: Place of the little church.
Killeevan: Church of St. Laobhan.
Killeglan: Church of the half-glen.
Killeigh: Church of the field.
Killelton: Church of St. Eiltin.
Killen: Little church.
Killenaule: Church of St. Naile.
Killenure: Corner of the yew tree.
Killerig: Church of St. Earc.
Killery: Red narrow sea-inlet.
Killeshin: Church of St. Oisin.
Killester: Church of St. Easra.
Killeter: Lower wood.
Killimer: Church of St. Iomar.
Killimor: Church of St. Iomar.
Killinaboy: Church of the daughter of Baoth.
Killinchy: Church of St. Duinseach.
Killiney: Church of the daughters of Leinin.
Killinick: Church of St. Finneog.
Killmakilloge: Church of St. Mocheallog.
Kill of the Grange: Church of the grange.
Killone: Church of St. John (the Baptist).
Killorglin: Church of St. Orgla.
Killough: Church of the lake.
Killowen: Church of St. John (the Baptist).
Killukin: Church of St. Eimhicin.

Killure: Church of the yew tree.

Killybegs: Little churches.

Killyclogher: Church of the stony place.

Killycluggin: Church of the little bell.

Killyclogher: Church of the stony place.

Killycolpy: Wood of the steer.

Killyfassy: Wood of the wilderness.

Killygarry: Short wood.

Killylergan: O'Ciaragan's wood.

Killylea: Grey wood.

Killyleagh: Church of the descendants of Laoch.

Killymacanoge: Church of St. Machonog.

Killynaher: Church of the father.

Killyon: Church of St. Leidhan.

Kilmacduagh: Church of son of Duach (St. Colman).

Kilmacow: Church of St. Mochua.

Kilmacreehy: Church of the sons of Creithe.

Kilmacrenan: Church of the sons of Neanan.

Kilmacthomas: Wood of little Thomas.

Kilmaine: Middle church.

Kilmainham: Church of St. Maighnenn.

Kilmalkedar: Church of St. Maolcheadar.

Kilmallock: Church of St. Mocheallog.

Kilmannock: Church of the monks.

Kilmeadan: Church of St. Miadan.

Kilmeedy: Church of St. Ide.

Kilmessan: Church of St. Measan.

Kilmichael: Church of St. Michael.

Kilmore: Big church.

Kilmovee: Church of St. Mobhi.

Kilmuckridge: Church of St. Mochraise.

Kilmurry: Church of Muire (Gaelic form of the Virgin's name).

Kilmurvey: Church of the shore.

Kilnalag: Church of the hollows.

Kilnaleck: Church of the flagstones.

Kilnamanagh: Church of the monks.

Kilnaraha: Church of the ring-fort.

Kilnasaggart: Church of the priests.

Kilnavert: Church of the graves.

Kilpatrick: Church of St. Patrick.

Kilpedder: Church of St. Peter.

Kilrane: Church of the ferns.

Kilrea: Russet church.

Kilree: Church of the king.

Kilreekill: Church of St. Richil.

Kilronan: Church of St. Ronan.

Kilronane: Church of St. Ronan.

Kilroot: Russet church.

Kilross: Church of the wood.

Kilsallagh: Willow wood.

Kilsaran: Wood of the parsnips.

Kilshanny: Church of St. Seanach.*

Kilsheelan: Church of St. Siolan.

Kilskeery: Church of St. Scire.

Kiltamagh: Church of the descendants of Laoch.

Kiltartan: Church of St. Tartan.

Kiltealy: Church of St. Sheila.

Kilteel: Church of St. Sheila.

Kiltegan: Church of St. Teagan.

Kilternan: Church of St. Tiarnan.

Kiltoom: Church of the burial mound.
Kiltubrid: Church of the well.
Killtullagh: Church of the little hill.
Kilturk: Wood of the boars.
Kiltyclogher: Woods of the stony place.
Kilwatermoy: Church of the upper plain.
Kilworth: Church of the order.
Kinawley: Church of St. Naile.
Kincaslagh: Head of the inlet.
Kincon: Hound's head.
Kincora: Weir head.
Kindrum: Head of the ridge.
Kingarrow: Rough head.
Kinlough: Head of the lake.
Kinnegad: Ford-head of the willow sticks or withes.
Kinneigh: Horse's head.
Kinnitty: Eitach's head.
Kinsale: Sea headland.
Kinvarra: Sea head.
Kinvoy: Head of the plain.
Kircubbin: Church of St. Goban.
Kishkeam: Bottom of the pass.
Knappagh: Hilly land.
Knockane: Little hill.
Knockacappul: Hill of the horse.
Knockacullen: Hill of the holly.
Knockalongy: Hill of the encampment.
Knockalough: Hill of the lake.
Knockamore: Big hill.
Knockanaffrin: Hill of the Mass.
Knockanillaun: Hill of the island.

Knockaraha: Hill of the ring-fort.

Knockaraven: Hill of the small bird.

Knockatemple: Hill of the church.

Knockatober: Hill of the well.

Knockatooa: Hill of the sorrel.

Knockaunapeebra: Little hill of the piper.

Knockbrack: Speckled hill.

Knockbrandon: Hill of St. Brendan.

Knockchree: Heart-shaped hill.

Knockcloghrim: Hill of the stony ridge.

Knockcroghery: Hill of the hangman.

Knockduff: Dark or black hill.

Knockeen: Little hill.

Knocklayd: Broad hill.

Knocklofty: Hill of the shelf.

Knocklong: Hill of the encampment.

Knockmahon: Hill of the river Mahon.

Knockmany: Middle hill.

Knockmaroon: Maolruan's hill.

Knockmealdown: Maoldomhnach's hill (lit., hill of the servant of the church).

Knockmore: Big hill.

Knockmoy: Muaidh's hill.

Knockmoyleen: Hill of the little plain.

Knocknaboola: Hill of the summer-pasture.

Knocknacarry: Hill of the weir.

Knocknafreaghaun: Hill of the bilberries.

Knocknagappul: Hill of the horses.

Knocknageeha: Hill of the wind.

Knocknageragh: Hill of the sheep.

Knocknagillagh: Hill of the woodcock.

Knocknahoo: Hill of the cave.
Knocknahorna: Hill of the barley.
Knocknalosset: Hill of the fertile spots.
Knocknamona: Hill of the bog.
Knocknanuss: Hill of the deer.
Knocknarea: Hill of the executions.
Knockpatrick: Hill of St. Patrick.
Knockrath: Hill of the ring-fort.
Knock Rua: Russet hill.
Knockrush: Hill of the wood.
Knockshee: Hill of the fairies/hill of the fairy mound.
Knocksouna: November hill (place of November celebrations).
Knocktemple: Hill of the church.
Knocktopher: Hill of the causeway.
Knopoge: Low hill.
Kyle: Church or wood.
Kylebeg: Small church or wood.
Kylemore (Galway): Great wood.
Kylesa: Church of Jesus.

Laban: Miry place.
Labasheeda: Sioda's bed.
Labba: Bed or grave.
Labbacallee: Hag's bed.
Labbamolaga: St. Molaga's bed.
Lack: Flagstone.
Lackagh: Place of flagstones.
Lackamore: Great hillside.
Lackan: Hillside.

Lagan: Small hollow or low-lying land.
Laght: Gravestone or monument.
Laghy: Muddy place.
Lagore: Horse lake.
Laharan: Half land.
Lahard: Half height; easy slope.
Lahardan: Easy hill-slope.
Lahinch: Half island or peninsula.
Lakyle: Half-wood.
Lambeg: Small church.
Laracor: Place of the weir.
Laragh: Site or place.
Largan: Side of the hill.
Largy: Slope.
Larne: District of Lahar (a legendary prince).
Latteragh: Wet hillsides.
Lavey: Place of elms.
Leabeg: Small grey place.
Leagh: Grey place.
Leamaneh: Horse's leap.
Leamlara: Mare's leap.
Leamore: Big grey place.
Lear: Fork formed by rivers or glens.
Lecale: Cahal's half.
Lecarrow: Half-quarter.
Leckanvy: Ainbhe's flagstone.
Leckaun: Hillside.
Leenane: Tidal area.
Legacurry: Hollow of the whirlpool.
Legananny: Hollow of the marsh.
Leggs: Hollows.

Legland: Half-glen.

Legoniel: Hollow of the lime (another possible meaning: O'Neill's Hollow).

Lehinch: Half-island or peninsula.

Leighlin: Half-glen.

Leinster: Place of broad spears ('ster' is Scandinavian and means 'place').

Leitrim: Grey ridge.

Leixlip: Salmon leap.

Lemanaghan: Grey place of St. Manachan.

Lemybrien: O'Brien's leap.

Letter: Wet hillside.

Letterbreen: Bruin's hillside.

Letterbrick: Breac's hillside.

Letterfinish: Hillside of white water.

Letterfrack: Frac's hillside.

Lettergarriv: Rough hillside.

Lettergow: Hillside of the smith (MacGowan).

Letterkenny: Hillside of the O'Ceananns.

Lettermacaward: Hillside of the son of the bard (MacWard).

Lettermore: Great hillside.

Lettermullan: Meallin's hillside.

Liffock: Small half.

Limavady: Leap of the dog.

Limerick: Bare land.

Lisball: Ring-fort of spots.

Lisballad: Ring-fort of the pass.

Lisbane: White ring-fort.

Lisbellaw: Ring-fort of the ford-mouth.

Lisburn: Ring-fort of the spring (originally: ring-fort of the gamblers).

Liscannor: Ceannur's ring-fort.

Liscarney: Cearnach's ring-fort.

Liscarroll: Cearbhall's ring-fort.

Liscartan: Cartan's ring-fort.

Lisclogher: Ring-fort of the stony place.

Liscloon: Sloping ring-fort.

Lisdoonvarna: The lios or enclosure of the gapped fort.

Lisduff: Black ring-fort.

Lisfinny: Finin's ring-fort.

Lisgall: Ring-fort of the foreigners.

Lisgoole: Ring-fort of the fork.

Lisheen: Little ring-fort.

Lislap: Ring-fort of the bed.

Lislaughlin: Ring-fort of St. Lachtin.

Lislea: Grey ring-fort.

Lismore: Great ring-fort.

Lisnalee: Ring-fort of the calves.

Lisnagreeve: Ring-fort of the branches.

Lisnagry: Ring-fort of the horse-breeding place.

Lisnagunogue: Ring-fort of the churns.

Lisnarrick: Ring-fort of the small oaks.

Lisnaskea: Ring-fort of the whitethorn trees (another possible meaning: Ring-fort of the shield).

Lispole: Paul's ring-fort.

Lisryan: Rian's ring-fort.

Liss: Ring-fort.

Lissan: Little ring-fort.

Lissadell: Ring-fort of the blind.

Lissard: High ring-fort.

Lissoughter: Upper ring-fort.
Lissoy: Ring-fort of the cave.
Lisselton: Eiltin's ring-fort.
Lissycasey: O'Casey's ring-fort.
Listellian: Teallan's ring-fort.
Listowel: Tuathal's ring-fort.
Lixnaw: Flagstone of the swimming.
Loghill: Elm wood.
Lohort: Garden (often as attached to a castle or fort).
Londonderry: Derry — oak grove (London was added under James I).
Longford: Fortress.
Loop Head: Leap head.
Loughan: Small place.
Loughanavally: Little lake of the road.
Loughanure: Lake of the yew tree.
Lough Beagh: Birch lake.
Loughbeg: Little lake.
Loughbrickland: Bricriu's lake.
Lough Conn: Lake of the hound.
Loughcrew: Lake of the branch.
Lough Cutra: Cutra's lake.
Lough Derg: Lake of the red eye.
Loughermore: Large district of rushes.
Lough Erne: Lake of the Erni (grouping of people).
Lough Esk: Lake of fish.
Lough Finn: White lake.
Loughgall: Bright lake.
Lough Gara: O'Gara's lake.
Loughill: Bright lake.
Lough Inagh: Ivy lake.

Loughinisland: Island lake.
Lough Melvin: Lake of Meilghe (a legendary king).
Lough Nafooey: Lake of the phantom.
Lough Neagh: Eochadh's lake.
Lough Oughter: Upper lake.
Loughrea: Grey lake.
Loughreagh: Brindled lake.
Lough Rosmore: Lake of the large peninsula.
Loughros: Rushy peninsula.
Lucan: Place of marsh-mallows.
Lug: Hole.
Lugatemple: Hole or hollow of the church.
Lugduff: Black hole.
Lugnaquilla: Hollow of the woodcocks (another possible meaning: Hollow of the wood).
Lurga: Strip of land.
Lurgan: Strip of land.
Lurganboy: Yellow strip of land.
Lurraga: Strip of land.
Lusk: Cave.
Lusty: A kneading trough; figuratively, a fertile field or place.
Lyracrompane: Fork of the creek.
Lyre: Fork.
Lyreboy: Yellow river-fork.

Maam: Elevated pass.
Maamturk: Pass of the boars.
Maas: A thigh, hill.
Macollop: Colpa's plain.

Maghancoosaun

Maghancoosaun: Milking-place of the little recess.

Maghanlawaun: Milking-place of the elm tree.

Maghera: Plain of the ring-fort.

Magherafelt: Rushy plain (another possible meaning: Plain of Fiolta's house).

Magheralin: Plain of the church (another possible meaning: Plain of the pool).

Magheramore: Great plain.

Magheravelly: Plain of the low ground.

Maghery: Plain.

Mahee Island: St. Mochaoi's island.

Malahide: Ide's hill-top.

Malone: Plain of meadows (another possible meaning: plain of lambs).

Mallow: Plain of the river Allo.

Malin: Brow, hill-brow.

Malinmore: Big hill-brow.

Mallaranny: Hill-brow of the ferns.

Malahide: Ide's hilltop.

Mandistown: Manda's town.

Manulla: Fionnalbha's plain.

Mashanaglass: Plain of the old stream.

Massareene: Hill of the queen.

Maul: Small hill.

Maumeen: Little mountain pass.

Maumore Gap: Great gap.

Maumturk: Mountain pass of the boars.

Mayglass: Green plain.

Maynooth: Nuadhat's plain.

Mayo: Plain of the yew trees.

Mayobridge: Bridge of the plain of the yew trees.

Maze: Plain.
Meen: Mountain-meadow.
Meenachan: Mountain-meadow of the son of Cathan.
Meenaclady: Mountain-meadow of the river Clady.
Meenagorp: Mountain-meadow of the bodies.
Meenaneary: Mountain-meadow of the shepherd.
Meenboy: Yellow mountain-meadow.
Meencarrigagh: Rocky mountain-meadow.
Meenkeeragh: Mountain-meadow of the sheep.
Merrion: Land along the sea shore.
Milleens: Small hills.
Moate: Mound.
Moher (Cliffs): Cliffs of the ruin.
Mohill: Soft land.
Moig: Plain.
Moira: Plain of the ring-forts.
Molana: St. Molana's abbey.
Monaghan: Place of thickets.
Monaincha: Bog of the island.
Monard: High bog.
Monasteranenagh: Monastery of the fair.
Monasterboice: St. Buithin's monastery.
Monasterevin: St. Eimhin's monastery.
Monasteroris: Feoras' monastery.
Monea: Plain of heroes.
Moneen: Small bog.
Moneydorragh: Night-dark grove.
Moneygall: Grove of the foreigners.
Moneyglass: Green grove.
Moneylea: Grey grove.
Moneymore: Great grove.

Moneyneany

Moneyneany: Bog of the wonders.
Mooghaun: Tunnell.
Mooncoin: Caidhn's bog.
Monroe: Russet bog.
Moroe: Russet plain.
Mosney: Muirid's plain.
Mountgarret: Gairead's castle.
Mountrath: Bog of the ring-fort.
Mourne Abbey: Abbey of the bog.
Movilla: Plain of the sacred tree.
Moville: Plain of the sacred tree.
Moy: Plain.
Moyard: High plain.
Moyarget: Plain of silver.
Moyarta: Plain of the grave.
Moyasta: Seasta's plain.
Moycullen: Plain of holly.
Moygannon: Plain of Ceanann.
Moygawnagh: Plain of the milch cows.
Moyle: Bare hill.
Moylett: Plain of grave stones.
Moylough: Lake plain.
Moymore: Great plain.
Moynalty: Plain of the flocks.
Moyne: Plain of the enclosure (abbey).
Moyra: Place abounding in salmon.
Moyrus: Plain of the peninsula.
Moytura: Plain of towers.
Moyvalley: Plain of the way.
Moyvilla: Plain of the sacred tree.
Moyvore: Moore's plain.

Muckamore: Plain of the confluence.
Muckanaght: Place of pigs.
Muckish: Pig back.
Muckloon: Pig meadow.
Muckross: Pig peninsula.
Muff: Plain.
Muineagh: Grove, brake.
Muings: Ferns or sedges.
Muldonagh: Sunday hill or church hill.
Mulhuddart: Eiderne's hilltop.
Mullabohy: Hilltop of the hut.
Mullacurry: Hilltop of the marsh.
Mullagh: Hilltop.
Mullaghanee: Hilltop of the deer.
Mullaghareirk: Hilltop of the outlook.
Mullaghboy: Yellow hilltop.
Mullaghmarakill: Great hilltop of the wood.
Mullaghmeen: Smooth hilltop.
Mullaghmore: Great hilltop.
Mullaghnaneane: Hilltop of the birds.
Mullaghroe: Russet hilltop.
Mullamast: Maiste's hilltop.
Mullan: Little summit.
Mullary: Lamhrach's plain.
Mullinahone: Mill of the cave.
Mullinavat: Mill of the stick.
Mullingar: Carr's mill.
Mully: Hilltop.
Mulnavannoge: Hill of the scald crows.
Mulrany: Ferny hill-brow.
Mulroy: Bare russet hill.

Multyfarnham: Farannan's mills.
Munster: Place of the men of Mumha.
Murneen: Agreeable place.
Murreagh: Flat marshy land by the sea.
Murrisk: Marsh by the sea.
Murroe: Russet plain.
Murrough: Russet plain.
Murrow: Marsh by the sea.
Murvey: Sea shore.
Muskerry: Descendants of Carbery Musc.
Mweelrea: Bare russet hilltop.
Myshall: Low plain.

Naas: A fair or meeting place.
Nad: Nest.
Nantinan: Place of nettles.
Nafooey (Lough): Lake of the phantom.
Navan: New habitation?
Ned: Nest.
Nenagh: The fair or assembly (of East Munster).
New Ross: Wood (of the son of Treon).
Newry: The yew tree at the head of the strand.
Newtownards: New town of the Ards (i.e., of the heights).
Newtownbreda: New town of the broken land.
Noard: New height.
Nobber: The work.
Nohoval: New habitation.
Nure: Yew tree.
Nurney: Oratory.

Offaly: Descendants of Ros of the rings (son of a legendary/historical king).

Oghermong: Swamp edge.

Oghill: Yew grove.

Ogonnelloe: District of the O'Connolly family.

Olderfleet Castle: Castle of Ulfrick's fjord.

Omagh: Virgin plain/sacred plain.

Omeath: Land of the descendants of Meith.

Oola: Apples or orchards.

Oran: Cold spring.

Oranmore: Big cold spring.

Oulart: Orchard.

Ovens: Caves.

Oughterard: High upper place.

Oughtmama: Upper pass.

Owbeg: Little river.

Owenass: River of the waterfall.

Owenbegs: Little river.

Owenboy (Owenbwee): Yellow river.

Owenea: River of the deer.

Owenglas: Green river.

Owenmore: Big river.

Owentocher: River of the causeway.

Ownagarry: River of the garden.

Ox Mountains: Mountain of the stones.

Oxmantown or Ostmantown: Town of the Ostmen or Danes.

Pallas: Palisade.

Pallasgreany: Caonrach's Palisade.

Pallaskenry: Caonrach's palisade.

Park: Field.
Parkalassa: Field of the ring-fort.
Parkmore: Great field.
Parknasilla: Field of the willows.
Pettigo: Place of the smith's house.
Phoenix: Bright or clear water.
Piltown: Town of the hole.
Pluck: Protuberance.
Pollacappul: Hole of the horse.
Pollaphuca: Hole of the Puca.
Pollremon: Redmond's hole.
Pollrone: Ruadhan's hole.
Pollsallagh: Hole of the willows.
Portacloy: Harbour of the wall.
Portadown: Landing place of the small fortress.
Portavogie: Harbour of the bog.
Port Ballintrae: Harbour of the town of the strand.
Portbraddon: Salmon harbour.
Portglenone: Fortress of the meadow of Eoghan.
Port Laoise: Fort of the descendants of Laois.
Portmarnock: Harbour of St. Mearnog.
Portmuck: Harbour of the pigs.
Portnablagh: Harbour of the buttermilk.
Portnashangan: Landing-place or river-bank of the ants.
Portnoo: New harbour.
Portora: Landing-place of the apple-trees.
Portraine: Port of Lambay (Reachrann Island).
Portroe: Russet fortress.
Portrush: Harbour of the headland.
Portsalon: Harbour of the salt.

Portumna: Landing-place of the tree trunk.
Poulaphouca: Hole or pool of the Puca.
Poulewhack: Hole of the angular space or river turn.
Poulgorm: Blue or dark hole.
Preban: Patch.
Puckaun: Little bag.

Quileagh: Chalky.
Quilty: Woods.
Quoile: Wood.

Raffeen: Smooth ring-fort.
Rahan: Ferny spot.
Raharney: Ring-fort of the alder tree.
Raheen: Little ring-fort.
Raheenduff: Little black ring-fort.
Raheny: Eanna's ring-fort.
Raholp: Ring-fort of the steer.
Ramelton: Mealtan's ring-fort.
Ramoan: Modhan's ring-fort.
Ramore: Great ring-fort.
Raphoe: Ring-fort of the huts.
Rasharkin: Earcan's wood or headland.
Ratallen: Ring-fort of salt.
Ratass: Southern ring-fort.
Rath: Ring-fort.
Rathangan: Ring-fort of the stronghold.
Rathclogh: Ring-fort of the stones.
Rathcoole: Cumhall's ring-fort.
Rathcormack: Cormac's ring-fort.
Rathcroghan: Cruachan's ring-fort.

Rathdangan: Ring-fort of the stronghold.
Rathdowney: Ring-fort of the church.
Rathdrinagh: Thorny ring-fort.
Rathdrum: Ring-fort of the ridge.
Rathduff: Black ring-fort.
Rathfarnham: Fearnan's ring-fort.
Rathfeigh: Ring-fort of the exercise green.
Rathfran: Black Bran's ring-fort.
Rathfriland: Fraoile's ring-fort.
Rathgar: Rough ring-fort.
Rathglass: Green ring-fort.
Rathgormuck: Cormac's ring-fort.
Rathkeale: Caola's ring-fort.
Rathkeevin: Kevin's ring-fort.
Rathkenny: Ceannach's ring-fort.
Rathlee: Ring-fort of the calves.
Rathmelton: Mealtan's ring-fort.
Rathmichael: Michael's ring-fort.
Rathmines: Maoinis' ring-fort.
Rathmolyon: Moladhan's ring-fort.
Rathmullan: Maolan's ring-fort.
Rathnew: Naoi's ring-fort.
Rathnure: Ring-fort of the yew tree.
Rathowen: Eoghan's ring-fort.
Rathumney: Ring-fort of the oak.
Rathvilla: Ring-fort of the sacred tree.
Rathvilly: Ring-fort of the sacred tree.
Rattoo: Northern ring-fort.
Ray: Ring-fort.
Reban: White flat-place on a hill.
Ree (Lake): Grey lake.

Reen: A land point.
Reenard: High headland.
Reenabenny: Point of the peak.
Rehins: Little forts.
Relagh: Flat part of a mountain.
Riesk: Marsh.
Rindown: Point of the fort.
Rineen: Little point of land.
Ring: Point of land, hill.
Ringabella: Headland of the sacred tree.
Ringaskiddy: Headland of the Skiddy family.
Ringville: Headland of the sacred tree.
Roeilaun: Russet island.
Roosky: Marshy place.
Rosbeg: Little headland.
Roscommon: St. Coman's wood.
Rosconnell: Conal's wood.
Roscor: Round promontory.
Roscrea: Cre's wood.
Rosenallis: Wood of the clear stream.
Rosguill: Goll's peninsula.
Roslea: Grey wood.
Rosmuc: Headland of pigs.
Rosmult: Wood of the wethers.
Rossard: High wood.
Rossbeigh: Birch headland.
Rosserk: Earc's headland.
Rosserrilly: Wood of the eastern pass.
Rosses: Headlands.
Rossglass: Green headland.
Rossin: Small wood.

Rossinver: Headland of the river-mouth.
Rosslare: Middle headland.
Rosslea: Grey headland.
Rossmore: Big wood.
Rossnowlagh: Wood of the apples.
Rossorry: Eastern headland.
Rossroe: Russet wood.
Rostellan: Dillon's wood.
Rostrevor: Treabhar's wood.
Rosturk: Boar headland.
Roughan: Russet land.
Roughty: (Glen of) the O'Ruachtan family.
Rousky: Marshy place.
Rower: Russet land.
Ruan: Russet land.
Rush: Wood.
Rush (Dublin): Headland of the yew trees.
Rusky: Marshy place.
Rylane: Green field for festivities and sports.

Saggart: House of St. Sacra.
Sallahig: Miry place.
Sallins: Willow groves.
Saltee Island: Salt patterns.
Santry: Old petty kingdom.
Saul: Barn.
Sawel: Barn.
Scalp: Cleft or chasm.
Scarawalsh: Clear shallow water.
Scarriff: Rough shallow ford.
Scartaglen: Grove of the valley.

Scarva: Rough shallow ford.

Schull: Place of scolbs (sticks for thatching): another possible meaning: School or schools: Scoil Mhuire or Schools of St. Mary.

Scraghy: Boggy or grassy place.

Screer: Furrow.

Scribbagh: Poor pasture land.

Scullogue Gap: Gap of the small farmers.

Seagoe: Seat of St. Gobha.

Seefin: Seat of Fionn (MacCumhail).

Seskilgreen: The sixth part (a land measure) of the Church of Grianna.

Seskin: Marsh.

Seskinore: Gray marsh.

Shanacashel: Old stone fort.

Shanaclogh: Old stone castle.

Shanagarry: Old garden.

Shanaglish: Old church.

Shanagolden: Old hill-shoulder.

Shannakea: Old quagmire.

Shanakiel: Old wood.

Shanakill: Old church.

Shanboagh: Old hut.

Shandon: Old fort.

Shankill: Old church.

Shanmullagh: Old hill summit.

Shannowen: Old river.

Shantallow: Old land.

Shantonagh: Old rampart.

Sharavogue: Bitter place.

Shee: Fairy hill.

Sheeffry Hills: Mountains of the fairy mansion.
Sheelin (Lake): Lake of the fairies.
Sheeroe: Russet fairy hill.
Shelburne: Descendants of Bran.
Shelmaliere: Descendants of Maolughra.
Sherkinis: Arcan's island.
Sheskin: Marsh.
Shillelagh: Descendants of Ealach.
Shimna River: River of the bullrushes.
Shinrone: Seat of the seal.
Shrone: Pointed hill (literally: a nose).
Shrule: Stream.
Sion: Fairy Hill.
Skeagh: Whitethorn bush.
Skegoneill: Whitethorn of the earl (another possible meaning: O'Neill's whitethorn).
Skehanagh: Place of whitethorns.
Skelligs: Rocks.
Skenakilla: Bush of the church.
Skerries: Sea rocks.
Skibbereen: Place of little boats.
Skreen: Shrine.
Slea Head: Mountain headland.
Sleatygraigue: Village near the hills.
Slemish: Mountain of Mis (a woman).
Slieve Anieran: Mountain of the iron.
Slievebane: White mountain.
Slievebeagh: Bith's mountain.
Slieve Bearnagh: Gapped mountain.
Slieve Bloom: Bladhma's mountain.
Slieve Callan: Callan's mountain.

Slieve Corragh: Rugged mountain.
Slieve Croob: Hoof mountain.
Slieve Donard: St. Domhanghart's mountain.
Slieve Fuad: Fuad's mountain.
Slieve Gullion: Holly mountain.
Slieve League: Mountain of the flagstones.
Slieve Mell-more: Great bare mountain.
Slieve Miskish: Mountain of enmity.
Slievenabrock: Mountain of the badgers.
Slieve Na Goill: Mountain of the woods.
Slievenamaddy: Mountain of the dogs.
Slievenamon: Mountain of the women.
Slievenamuck: Mountain of the pigs.
Slieve Reagh: Gray mountain.
Slieve Roe: Russet mountain.
Slieverue: Russet mountain.
Slieve Snaght: Mountain of the snow.
Sligo: Shelly river.
Sluggary: Quagmire.
Snave: Swimming place.
Sneem: Knot.
Solloghod: Willow wood.
Sonnagh: Mount or rampart.
Spancel Hill: Hill of the cold wood.
Speenoge: Place of gooseberry bushes.
Spelga Pass: Pass of the pointed rock.
Sperrin Mountains: Pointed hills.
Spiddal: Hospital.
Spike Island: Island of the Picts.
Spink: Pointed cliff or rock.
Sragh (Srah): River-meadow.

Srahlea: Gray river-meadow.
Srahmore: Big river-meadow.
Srahnalong: River-meadow of the ships.
Srahnamanragh: River-meadow of the enclosures or pounds.
Staholmog: House of St. Calmoc.
Staigue: Strip of land.
Stamullin: House of Maelin.
Stillorgan: House of St. Lorcan.
Strabane: White river-meadow.
Stradbally: Village, one-street town.
Strade: Street.
Stradone: Deep river-meadow.
Straffan: Little stream.
Stragolan: Sand-bottom fork.
Straidarran: O'Aran's village.
Strancally: Hag's nose.
Strangford: Strong-flowing fjord.
Stranmillis: Sweet stream.
Stranoodan: Nuodan's river-meadow.
Stranorlar: River-meadow of the floor or level place.
Stroove: Stream.
Struell: Stream.
Sturrall Promontory: Promontory of the pinnacle.
Suil: Eye.
Swords: Sword (of St. Colmcille).
Sylaun: Place of willows.

Tacumshane: House of St. Coimshin.
Taghadoe: House of St. Tua.
Taghmon: House of St. Munna.

Tagoat: House of St. Cod.

Tallaght: Plague grave.

Tallow: Land (another possible meaning: hill).

Tamlaght: Plague grave.

Tanderagee: Back to the wind, leeward.

Tamnamore: Large arable place in a less fertile district.

Tamney: Green or arable area in a less fertile district.

Tang: Tongue.

Tara: Assembly place.

Tarbert: Neck of land.

Tarmon: Sanctuary, church land.

Tattymoyle: Bare land area (about sixty acres).

Taughmonagh: Territory of the Manaigh (a people).

Tawlaght: Plague burial place.

Tecolm: House of St. Colm.

Tedavnet: House of St. Dympna.

Templeboy: Church of St. Baoth.

Templebreedy: Church of St. Brigid.

Templederry: Church of the oak grove.

Templeglentan: Church of the little glen.

Templemichael: Church of St. Michael.

Templemolaga: Church of St. Molaga.

Templemonachan: Church of St. Monachan.

Templemore: Big church.

Templenoe: New church.

Templeogue: Church of St. Maolog.

Templepatrick: Church of St. Patrick.

Templeshanbo: Church of the old hut of Sin (man's name).

Tempo: The (right-hand) turn.

Terenure: Land of the yew tree.
Termon: Sanctuary, church land.
Termonbarry: Church-land of St. Bearach.
Termonfeckin: Church-land of St. Feichin.
Terryglass: Land of the two streams.
Tevrin: Little hill.
Thomond: North Munster.
Thurles: Strong ring-fort.
Tieve: Hillside.
Tildarg: Red land.
Timoleague: House of St. Molaga.
Timolin: House of St. Moling.
Tinamuck: House of the pigs.
Tinahely: House of the river Ely.
Tinnahinch: House of the river-meadow.
Tipperary: House of the well of Ara (an old district).
Tirawly: Land of Amhalgadh.
Tirconnell: Land of Conal.
Tirkerran: Land of Caerthann.
Tirnaneill: Land of the descendants of Niall.
Tober: Well.
Toberboe: Well of the cows.
Tobercurry: Well of the cauldron or whirlpool.
Toberdoney: Well of the church (Tobereendoney: Well of the King of Sunday, that is, God).
Tobermoney: Well of the shrubbery.
Tobermore: Large well.
Toberroe: Russet well.
Togher: Causeway.
Tollymore: Large hill.
Tomdeely: Burial mound of the river Deel.

Tomies: Mountain of the burial mound.
Tonregee: Back to the wind; leeward.
Toolclae: Clae's district or petty kingdom.
Toombeola: Beola's burial mound.
Toome: Burial mound.
Toomyvara: Burial mound of O'Meara.
Tooreen: Little bleach-green.
Toormore: Large bleach-green.
Torc Mountain: Mountain of the boar.
Tormore: Tower-like rock.
Torr Head: Pointed hill.
Tory: Tower-like rock.
Toureen: Little bleach-green.
Tourmakeady: Bleach-green of the son of Eadach.
Trabane: White strand.
Tralee: Strand of Li.
Tramore: Great strand.
Tranarossan: Strand of the groves.
Trasna Island: Island across the passage.
Trawbreaghaboy: Treacherous strand.
Trean: Third part.
Trillick: Three flagstones.
Trim: Ford of the elder bushes.
Trostan: Pilgrim's staff (a hill shape).
Trough: Thirty hundreds of land, a barony.
Trumman: Place of elder bushes.
Truskmore: Great cod.
Tuam: Grave mound.
Tuamgraney: Grave mount of Grian.
Tubber: Well.
Tubbercurry: Well of the cauldron or whirlpool.

Tubbrid

Tubbrid: Well.
Tulla: Little hill.
Tullaghan: Little hill.
Tullaherin: Dry little hill.
Tullaghogue: Little hill of the youths.
Tullamore: Big hill.
Tullaroon: Little russet hill.
Tullig: Little hill.
Tullow: Little hill.
Tully: Little hill.
Tullybeg: Little hill.
Tullyhogue: Little hill of the youths.
Tullydonnell: Donal's little hill.
Tullyhomman: Little hill of the hollow (another possible meaning: Hill of the Timmons family).
Tullynagrow: Little hill of the cattle huts.
Tullyrap: Little hill of the fragments.
Tulrohaun: Little hill of the stream.
Tumna: Grave mound of the woman.
Ture: Yew tree.
Turlough: A lake that dries up in summer.
Turloughmore: Big lake that dries up in summer.
Tuskar: Rock.
Tybraughney: Braichne's house.
Tyholland: Talan's house.
Tymon: Modhichon's house.
Tyone: Eoghan's house.
Tyrella: House of St. Riaghal.
Tyrone: Descendants of Eoghan.

Ullard: Heights.

Ulster: Place of the men of Ulaid.
Urlanmore: Great forecourt.
Urbalreagh: Gray dell.
Urlar: Level place.
Urlingford: Ford of the slaughter.
Urris: Peninsula.
Urrisbee: Yellow peninsula.
Ushnagh: Place of fawns.

Valentia: Mouth of the island.
Vartry: Men of the land.
Veagh: Birch lake.
Ventry: White strand.
Vinegar Hill: Hill of the wood of the berries.

Waterford: Vadre fjord/Vedrefiordr.
Wexford: West fjord.

Youghal: Yew wood.

Glossary of Root Words

The place-names in this book form only a small part of all those that exist. For that reason the little glossary of root words that follows may be of use to those who want a minimal 'do-it-yourself' guide. Etymology in deciphering place-names can be misleading but it is helpful much more often than not. Moreover, these root words may help readers to make out components of the names that have been given in the preceding lists. Finally, the word forms given in italics represent ways in which the Irish words have been anglicised — and often these English versions convey the Irish sounds or a rough approximation of them.

ABHA (*Aw, ow, owen*): A river, stream.

ACHADH (*Agh, agha, augh*): A field, land, plain.

AILL (*Aile, aill, aul*): A cliff, rock.

ÁLT (*Alt*): A ravine, gully, wooded glen, mountain.

AIREAGAL (*arrigle, errigal*): A cell, oratory.

ÁIT (Combines with *teach* (house) in place-names: the combination is found as *att, atti, atty*): A place, locality.

AITEANN (*Attin, attina*): Gorse, furze.

ÁR (*Aar, are, air*): Slaughter.

ÁRD (*Ar, ard, ards*): A hill, high ground, top, high.

AONACH (*Enagh, eanig, eena*): An assembly, fair.

ÁTH (*A, aha, ath*): A ford.

BADHÚN (*Bawn*): An enclosure, a building surrounded by a fortification.

BAILE (*Bal, bally, vally*): A townland, town, village, homestead.

BÁN (*Bane, baun, vaun*): White, fair.

BÁRR (*Bar, barr, baur*): A top.

BEAG (*Beg*): Small.

BÉAL (*Bel, bell*): This word is commonly joined with 'Áth' to form Béal átha: Ford-mouth or Ford-approach (*Ball, bally, bella*). It is often difficult to distinguish it from '*Baile*': A mouth, opening, entrance.

BEALACH (*Ballagh, vally*): A road, way, mountain pass, inlet.

BEALTAINE (*Bedlam, beltany*): The month of May, the first day of May, May festival.

BEAN (*Ban, mna*): A woman.

83

BEANN (*Ban, ben, bin*): A point, headland, peak.

BEANNACHAIR (*Banagher, bangor*): Abounding in peaks.

BEÁRNA (*Barna, barnet, varna*): Gap, defile, chasm.

BEITH (*Beagh, beha, behy*): A birch tree.

BILE (*Bella, villa, villy*): A sacred tree or grove, common as a religious place among Celtic peoples.

BÓ (*Bo, boe, moe*): A cow.

BOTH (*Bo, boha, ude*): A hut or tent.

BÓTHAR (*Batter, boher, voher*): A way, road.

BRUGH (*Brough, bru, brugh*): A mansion, palace, fort, fairy dwelling.

BUAILE (*Boley, boola, vooly*): An enclosure for milking cows; a place where cattle were driven to pasture in the summer season, especially in mountain or bog areas.

BUIDHE (*Boy, bwee*): Yellow.

BUN (*Bon, bun, bunn*): Bottom, foot.

CAISEAL (*Cashel, castle*): A bulwark, circular stone fort, stone building.

CAOIN (*Kean, keen*): Gentle, smooth, pleasing.

CAOL (*Keel, kil*): Narrow, slender.

CAORA (*Keera, keeragh, nageeragh*): A sheep, ewe.

CAPALL (*Capple, cappul, gappul*): A horse.

CARN (*Carn, carna*): A heap, cairn.

CARRAIG (*Carrick, carrig, carriga*): A rock, crag.

CATHAIR (*Caher, cahir*): A city, court, circular stone fort, principal church.

CEANN (*Kan, ken, kin*): A head.

CEAPACH (*Cap, cappa, cappagh*): A plot of land

laid out for tillage, denuded wood, reclaimed land.

CEATHRAMHADH (*Carhoo, carrow, kerry*): A fourth, quarter of land, quarter of a townland.

CÉIDE (*Keadagh, keadew, keady*): A plateau, flat-topped hill, assembly.

CILL (*Kil, kill, keel*): A church, churchyard, monastic cell.

CLANN (*Clan, clann, clanna*): Children, sept, followers.

CLÁR (*Clar, clare*): A level surface, flat country, plain.

CLOCH (*Clogh, clough, clohy*): A stone, stone castle.

CLOCHÁN (*Cloghan, cloghane, cloghaun*): A ruin, remains of old fort, townland containing parish church, stepping stones.

CLOCHAR (*Clogh, clogher*): A stone building, convent, church.

CLUAIN (*Clon, cloon, cloony*): A meadow, plain.

CNOC (*Crock, knock*): A hill, height, mountain.

COILL (*Cull, kil, kyle*): A wood, grove.

COINICÉAR (*Congykeare, conicar, nicker*): A rabbit warren.

CORA (*Cor, corra, curra*): A weir.

CORR (*Cor, corr, curr*): A conical hill, promontory.

COS (*Cosh, cush, cuss*): Foot.

CRANN (*Cran, crin, nagran*): A tree.

CROM (*Crom, croom, crum*): Bent, stooped, curved.

CROS (*Cros, crush, crusha*): A cross, cross-road, market place.

CRUACH (*Crogh, croagh, croghan*): A heap, symetrically shaped mountain.

CÚ (*Con, cu, nagon*): A Hound, fierce dog.

CÚIL (*Col, cool, cul*): A corner, nook.

CUIRREACH (*Curra, curragh, curry*): Moor, race-course, marsh.

CÚM (*Coom, combe, coum*): A waist, valley, coomb.

CUMAR (*Comber, cumber, cummer*): River, river-confluence, river-bed.

DAINGEAN (*Dangan, dingle*): Stronghold, fortress.

DEARG (*Darrig, dere, derg*): Red.

DEASMHUMHA (*Desmond*): South Munster, Des-mond.

DOIRE (*Der, derri, derry*): Oak tree, oak grove, wood.

DOMHNACH (*Don, donagh, dun*): Sunday, church.

DONN (*Don. donagh, dun*): Brown, brown-haired.

DROICHEAD (*Drehid, droghed, drohid*): Bridge, especially a stone bridge.

DROM (*Drim, drom, drum*): A back, shoulders, ridge.

DUBH (*Doo, duff, duv*): Black.

EACH (*Agh, augh, eigh*): Horse.

EAGLAIS (*Aglish, eglis, eglish*): Church.

EANACH (*Anna, annagh, anny*): Watery place, fen, marsh.

EAS (*Ass, assy, ess*): Waterfall, rapids.

EO (*O, oe, yo*): A yew tree.

FADA (*Ad, adda, fad*): Long.

FAILL (*Fall, foil, foyle*): Cliff.

FAITHCHE (*Faha, fahy, feigh*): A lawn, exercise green, playing-field.

FÁL (*Fal, falls*): Hedge, enclosure, pailing.

FEARANN (*Farn, farran, arran*): Land, ploughland.

FEARN (*Farn, farnagh, navern*): Alder tree.

FIODH (*Fee, feigh, fi*): Tree, wood.

FIONN (*Fin, finn, inn*): White, fair, beautiful.

FRAOCH (*Freagh, free, ree*): Heath, heather.

GABHA (*Gow, gown, gowan*): Smith.

GABHAL (*Gole, goole, goul*): Fork, junction, estuary.

GALL (*Gal, gall, gaul*): Foreigner.

GAOTH (*Gwee*): Inlet of the sea, sand stream.

GAOTH (*Gee, geeha, geehy*): Wind.

GARBH (*Garra, garriff, garve*): Rough, rugged.

GARRDHA; GARRAIDHE (*Gar, garra, garry*): Garden, enclosure.

GEAL (*Gal, gil, gilly*): White, bright, fair.

GLAS (*Glas, glass, glash*): Green, grey.

GLEANN (*Glan, glen, glanna*): Glen, hollow.

GORT (*Gart, gort, gurt*): Field, plantation.

GRÁIG (*Grag, graigue, greg*): Village, hamlet.

GRIANÁN (*Greenan, greenaun, grennan*): Summer dwelling, sun-bower.

INIS (*Inch, innis, innish, heensha*): Island, river-meadow, peninsula.

IUBHAR (*Ure, nure*): Yew tree, yew grove.

LADHAR (*Lyre, lear*): Fork of rivers or valleys.

LAG (*Lag, lig, lug*): Hollow, pool.

LANN (*Lan, lann, lyn*): A house, church.

LEABA (*Labba, labby*): A bed, grave.

LEAC (*Lack, leck, league*): A hard surface, stone, flagstone, tombstone.

LEACA (*Lacka, lackaun, leckan*): A flat sloping surface, brow of hill.

LEATHAN (*Lahan, lane*): Wide, broad.

LÉIM (*Leam, lem, lim*): A leap.

LEITIR (*Letter, lattera, letteragh*): A side of a hill, cliff, wet hillside.

LIAG (*Leg, legaun*): A boulder, flat stone, pillar stone.

LIATH (*Lea, leagh*): Grey, white.

LIOS (*Lis, lish, lassa*): A ring-fort, fairy rath.

LOCH (*Loch, lough, low*): A lake, pool, sea-islet.

LONG (*Long*): Ship.

MAC (*Ma, mac, mack*): A son, descendant.

MACHAIRE (*Maghera, maghery, vaghera*): A plain, battlefield.

MAGH (*Ma, may, moy*): A plain, battle-field.

MÁM (*Mam, maam, maum*): A mountain pass, summit.

MAOL (*Meel, mweel, moyle*): Bald, bare.

MÍN (*Min, meen*): Smooth, gentle, fine pasture, smooth spot on a mountain.

MÓIN (*Mona, mone, voone*): A moor, peat-bog.

MÓR (*Mor, more, moore*): Great, big, extensive.

MUC (*Muc, muck, mucky*): Pig.

MULLACH (*Mul, mullagh, mully*): Summit, height.

NUA (*New, noe*): New, recent.

Ó, UA (*O', y, ee*): A grandson, descendant.

POLL (*Foyle, poll, poul*): A hole, hollow.

PORT (*Fort, port*): A shore, harbour, ferry, passage, landing place.

PÚCA (*Puck, pooka, phuca*): Pooka, Puck, hobgoblin (a sprite who in the Celtic tradition embodies wayward or mischievous chance, on the whole benign and not evil).

RÁTH (*Ra, rath, raha*): A rath, fort, outer palisade of a lios.

RAITHÍN (*Raheen, raine, ramsy*): Bracken.

RIN (*Reen, rin, ring*): A point, promontory.

ROS (*Ros, ross, rush*): A wood, copse, promontory (mostly means a wood in the South and a peninsula in the North).

RUADH (*Red, roe, rua*): Russet, reddish-brown, foxcolour.

SAGART (*Saggart, taggart*): A priest.

SCEACH (*Skeagh, skehy, skew*): A thorn-bush, whitethorn.

SEAN (*Shan, shanna*): Old.

SEISLEANN (*Seskin, sheskin*): A marsh, miry place.

SLIABH (*Sle, slieve, tlieve*): A mountain, mountainous district, moorland.

SLIGHE (*Slee*): A way, road.

SRUTH (*Srue, sruh, srough*): Stream.

STRUTHAR (*Shruel, shrule, struell*): Stream, fast stream.

TEARMANN (*Termon*): Church land, termon, sanctuary.

TIGH (*Ta, tee, ti*): House, building.

TÍR (*Tir, tier*): Land, district, people.

TOBAR (*Tibret, tober, tubbrid*): Well.

TOR (*Tor*): Tower, mansion.

TORC (*Torc, turc*): Boar.

TRÁIGH (*Tra, traw, tray*): Strand, shore.

TUAR (*Tore, toor, tour*): Land, field, lea, bleach-green.

TULACH (*Tullagh, tullow, tully*): A small hill, mound.

UBHALL (*Aval, ool, owl*): An apple, orchard.

UISCE (*Isk, iska, isky*): Water.